Great People of the BIBLE

Catechist Guide

25 Easy-to-Use Sessions for Teaching Salvation History

Alan J. Talley

saint mary's press

The publishing team included Virginia Halbur and Brian Singer-Towns, development editors; prepress and manufacturing coordinated by the production departments of Saint Mary's Press.

Copyright © 2010 by Saint Mary's Press, Christian Brothers Publications, 702 Terrace Heights, Winona, MN 55987-1320, www.smp.org. All rights reserved. Permission is granted to reproduce only the materials intended for distribution to the students. No other part of this book may be reproduced by any means without the written permission of the publisher.

Printed in the United States of America

2306

ISBN 978-0-88489-869-6

Contents

Introduction 4
1. Salvation History 9
2. Introduction to the Old Testament 16
3. Adam and Eve 23
4. Noah 30
5. Abraham and Sarah 35
6. Moses 40
7. Joshua 46
8. Samson 51
9. Ruth 56
10. David 61
11. Solomon 67
12. Isaiah 72
13. Ezekiel 77
14. Ezra and Nehemiah 82
15. The Maccabees 87
16. Introduction to the New Testament 92
17. Mary of Nazareth 98
18. John the Baptist 103
19. Jesus and His Family 108
20. Jesus, Teachings and Miracles 113
21. Jesus, Death and Resurrection 120
22. Peter 126
23. Mary Magdalene 132
25. Paul 137
25. Priscilla and Aquila 143
Appendix: Answer Key 148

No part of the student workbook may be reproduced by any means.

Introduction

Great People of the Bible

Welcome to *Great People of the Bible Catechist Guide: Twenty-five Easy-to-Use Sessions for Teaching Salvation History*. These interactive sessions will help your young people grow in awareness of salvation history, as well as develop biblical literacy. The sessions introduce the participants to important Bible people and topics, showing how they fit into God's loving plan for our salvation. The catechist guide's easy-to-follow instructions enable volunteer catechists to connect Bible stories to Church teachings and to help the students connect those teachings with their daily lives.

Tips for Leading Sessions

Great People of the Bible Catechist Guide has been designed to make the catechist's preparation for leading sessions straightforward and as simple as possible. This section will walk you through planning a typical session, providing you with important background and tips for using the sessions effectively.

Session Time Frame

This catechist's guide has been created for 60-minute sessions. To use all the session components included here, the participants should complete the appropriate student textbook background sheet and activity page at home before each session. (If your class sessions are 75 minutes long, the participants could begin work on the background sheets and activity pages at the end of each session to prepare for the next session.) This approach has several benefits, as follows:

- The participants will begin sessions with a base of knowledge.
- They will carry into the home the lessons and information they learn about the Bible.
- They won't miss out on any of the session activities included in this guide.

Consider informing parents of your expectation that the participants come to sessions having completed the assigned student textbook pages. You can hold an introductory parent meeting, use e-mail, or send an announcement home with the participants.

Alternative Option

If requiring at-home work is not possible, you may skip the Bible Story Sharing in each session and allow the participants to read the background sheets in class. You can then encourage them to complete each session's activity page—a puzzle—at home after the session. If you take this approach, look for the Note Alternative Option reminders throughout the sessions. Suggestions for completing the reading in class may be found in Suggestions for Reading Together, found later in this introduction.

Materials and Preparation

Besides becoming familiar with the session steps and activities, you will need minimal advance preparation for the sessions. For example, you may need to gather supplies, make photocopies of handouts, and do some background reading. This preparation is outlined at the beginning of each session under the heading Materials and Preparation.

Quick-Start Activity

The first thing under Session Steps in each session is the Quick-Start Activity. These simple activities engage the participants with something fun and intriguing while they wait for the session to begin. You may write the directions on the board before the participants arrive, leaving you free to greet the participants as they arrive and to recruit volunteers. In each session the Quick-Start Activity is referred to again later in the Integration Activity.

Prayer Times

Each session begins and ends with a short prayer time. Young adolescents respond well to ritual, so the opening prayer always begins with a candle bearer and Bible bearer processing in and proclaiming the words, "Let us remember that we are in the holy presence of God."

Another ritual element is a special prayer space in your meeting area where the participants can gather for the opening and closing prayers. Your prayer space could consist of a table with a nice tablecloth or other covering and a Bible stand. If possible, create a space where the Bible may be displayed during the sessions, along with a portrait of the Bible person the class is studying, created by students during the first session. (See session 1, "Salvation History," for instructions for completing this activity.)

The participants should be involved in the prayer times as much as possible. If they are willing and able, they can read the Scripture passages and prayers, even if the directions do not call for volunteer readers.

Bible Story Sharing

The Bible Story Sharing part of each session helps the participants become familiar with using the Bible and connecting the lives of the Bible people with their own lives. This sharing begins with a reading from the Sacred Scriptures about the Bible person or topic. (See Suggestions for Reading Together, on the following page, for ways to have the participants read the Sacred Scriptures aloud.)

After the reading you will lead a discussion using three questions as a guide. The first question checks whether the participants have understood the passage. The second question helps the participants place themselves in the story in some way. The third question helps the participants see a connection between the Bible person's life and their own lives. Bible Story Sharing ends with a brief statement that summarizes the central teaching or connection that emerges from the passage.

Note Alternative Option: Omit Bible Story Sharing if you choose to have the participants read the background sheets in their student textbooks during the session. Instead of sharing, the participants would use this time to complete the reading. You may wish to use the techniques outlined in Suggestions for Reading Together.

Review Student Textbook Activity Page

During this part of the session, you will review the materials in the student textbook that the participants completed at home before the session. This material includes a background sheet with information about the Bible person or topic and an activity page. An answer key for the puzzles on the activity pages is included in the appendix at the back of this catechist's guide. You may check the activity pages in a number of ways:

- Simply read the answers to the participants.

- Call on participants to provide their answers.

- Choose a different participant to lead the review for each session.

- Invite the participants to swap books and check each other's work.

- Let the participants share and correct their work in small groups of three or four.

Note Alternative Option: Omit this part of the session if you choose to have the participants complete the activity pages at home after the session.

After checking the activity pages, you will briefly summarize the main points about the Bible person or topic. These points, highlighting key ideas from the background sheets, are listed for you in this catechist guide.

Integration Activity

The Integration Activity helps the participants gain a deeper understanding of salvation history and incorporate the lessons of the Bible into their daily lives. The Integration Activity generally begins with a discussion about the Quick-Start Activity. That discussion leads into an activity about a specific teaching based on the session's topic. Recognizing that every young adolescent learns differently, these activities use one or more of the following teaching techniques: drama, hands-on activities, physical movement, mental challenges, and creativity.

The Integration Activity generally ends by further helping the participants connect what they have just learned to their daily lives.

Announcements and Closing Prayer

The Announcements and Closing Prayer provide you with time to make announcements, as well as to assign the background sheets and activity pages as homework for the next session. A suggested simple closing prayer is also included.

Suggestions for Reading Together

Each session includes the reading of passages from the Sacred Scriptures. Remind the participants of the reverence and respect needed when the Scriptures are read. You may also ask the participants to read the student textbook background sheets during the session. Encourage the participants to read slowly and loudly and assure them that you will help with pronunciation as needed. The participants may read together in a variety of ways:

- Ask for a different volunteer to read aloud each session.
- Have each participant read a verse or sentence in turn.
- Ask several volunteers to read paragraphs in turn.
- If the passage is a narrative with several characters speaking, ask one participant to be the narrator and others to be the characters.
- Read the passage in echo fashion. To do this, you read a line, and the participants repeat it after you.

Resources

Essential Resources

The following two resources are used in the sessions and should be available during class:

- *Great People of the Bible.* This is the student textbook, containing background sheets and activity pages.
- *Breakthrough! The Bible for Young Catholics* or another Catholic Bible. Some sessions include suggestions for using the articles found in the *Breakthrough!* Bible. If you use another Bible, consider using the Good News Translation (GNT), which is age-apropriate, or the New American Bible (NAB), which is the basis for the *Lectionary.*

Recommended Resources

Saint Mary's Press offers other resources to supplement the sessions:

- *Breakthrough! The Bible Board Game.* Travel through various biblical eras (primeval history to early Christianity), answering questions about people of the Bible that address the who, where, when, what, how, and why of their places in salvation history. Players determine the length of time and game play by choosing from any of the designated starting and stopping points on the board—for example, the Garden of Eden, Egypt, the Promised Land, and the Temple—with New Jerusalem as the final destination. The team or individual who collects the most character cards wins the game.
- *Breakthrough! The Bible for Young Catholics Bible People Flash Cards*
  These flash cards are trading-sized cards that will help young adolescents learn about Bible people and events.
- *Bible Literacy Made Easy*
  This practical guide provides catechists, teachers, and youth ministers with the background necessary to form biblically literate young adolescents. In just a few hours, leaders will learn to teach the ABCs of biblical literacy to young people as follows:

- **Access:** Help young people become knowledgeable and comfortable in using the Bible.

- **Big picture:** Help young people know and understand the biblical story of salvation history.

- **Context:** Help young people understand how to interpret Bible books and passages in their proper contexts.

- *Saint Mary's Press Essential Quick Chart: Bible People*
  This chart provides an overview of thirty-three key people in the Bible. From Adam and Eve in the Old Testament to Priscilla and Aquila of the New Testament, this chart of Bible people shows how their lives point to or radiate from Jesus, the epicenter of salvation history.

Appendix: Answer Key

The appendix, found at the end of this catechist guide, contains the answer key for the puzzles that appear on the activity pages of *Great People of the Bible*.

Final Thoughts

Before you begin this exciting journey through salvation history with your young people, allow us to thank you for your willingness to hand on the faith tradition and help make it relevant to the lives of your young adolescents. Through your efforts these young people can grow in their love for the Sacred Scriptures and discover their own place in God's loving plan for our salvation. By helping them find their own story in the stories of the Bible people, you are giving them a gift that will last them a lifetime.

Chapter 1

Salvation History

Session Focus

- The participants will learn key facts about salvation history:

  - It is the story of how God saves us from sin and death and brings us to eternal life because of God's great love for us.

  - It spans both the Old and New Testaments.

  - It culminates in the life, Passion, death, and Resurrection of Jesus Christ.

  - Through our faith the story of salvation history becomes part of our own story, because God's plan is for us to have eternal life.

- The participants will briefly study the stories of each of the Bible people and reflect on key questions:

  - What unique qualities does each Bible person display?

  - Which Bible people are already familiar, and which do you look forward to learning more about?

At a Glance

A. Quick-Start Activity: Favorite Family Vacation (5 minutes)

B. Opening Prayer Ritual (5 minutes)

C. Bible Story Sharing: Jesus, the Way to the Father (10 minutes)

D. Review Student Textbook Activity Page (10 minutes)

E. Integration Activity: The People of Salvation History (25 minutes)

F. Announcements and Closing Prayer (5 minutes)

Materials and Preparation

Materials Needed

For each participant:

❏ Bible and student textbook

❏ pencil

- ❏ handout 1–A, "Bible Person's Picture Frame"
- ❏ colored pencils or crayons

Additional materials:

- ❏ tape

Other Preparation Steps

- ❏ Mark Luke 1:1–4 in the Bible that will be used in the opening prayer ritual.
- ❏ Choose two participants to process in with the Bible and a candle for the opening prayer ritual, providing directions as needed.
- ❏ Make a copy of resource 1–A, "Bible People," and cut it into strips.

Background Reading

- Read the background page about salvation history on page 6 of the student textbook, including the suggested Bible passages.

Session Steps

A. Quick-Start Activity: Favorite Family Vacation (5 minutes)

1. **Write** the following on the board:

   - Pair up with someone in the class and share a story about your favorite family vacation or trip. Once you have both shared your stories, find a new person to pair up with and share your stories. Keep switching partners until you have talked with everybody in the class or until I say time is up.

2. As the participants arrive, **instruct** them to follow the directions on the board.

B. Opening Prayer Ritual (5 minutes)

1. **Direct** the Bible bearer and candle bearer to take their places just outside the room or in the back of the room. **Gather** everyone else to stand around your prayer table. **Make** the Sign of the Cross and lead everyone in saying, "Let us remember that we are in the holy presence of God."

2. **Invite** the Bible bearer and candle bearer to silently process up to the prayer table and turn to face the group. The Bible bearer then **reads** the Scripture verse you have marked, Luke 1:1–4. When finished, the reader says, "The Word of the Lord." Everyone responds, "Thanks be to God." The Bible bearer and candle bearer then place the Bible and candle on the prayer table and go to their places.

3. Invite everyone to sit down. **Introduce** salvation history with these or similar words:

   ▶ During this course we will explore many different and amazing people found in the Bible. These people have laid the foundation for the faith we profess today. We will hear stories of great faith and great weakness, but all the stories tell how God worked through these people's lives to fulfill God's plan for humanity. Together all these stories find their meaning in one person, Jesus Christ, who brought salvation to the world. The individual stories are part of a bigger story, the story of salvation history. We will explore that big picture today.

C. Bible Story Sharing: Jesus, the Way to the Father (10 minutes)

Note Alternative Option: Omit step C if you choose to have the participants read the background sheet in the student textbook during class. Instead, the participants would use the time to complete the reading. You may wish to use the methods outlined in Suggestions for Reading Together, in the introduction to this catechist guide.

1. **Direct** the participants to open their Bibles to John 14:1–7. Provide help as needed but encourage the participants to find the passage on their own. **Read** the passage together. See the introduction in this catechist guide for different ways to do this.

2. **Lead** the group in a short reflection on the Bible passage. Encourage all the participants to share their thoughts.

   ▶ Where is Jesus going to prepare a place for the disciples? Why? *(Answer: Jesus says he is going to his Father's house to prepare a place for them so Jesus, the Father, and all of them may be together.)*

   ▶ When you think of Jesus preparing a place for you in Heaven, what do you imagine?

   ▶ How should a person live in order to enter Heaven?

3. **Summarize** the meaning of this Bible passage in these or similar words:

   ▶ It can be fun to think about Heaven. Jesus' description of the Father's house gives us a wonderful image of what Heaven will be like: a welcoming place where God the Father lives with the people and the people live in unity and peace forever with Jesus. Living in perfect peace with God and one another is a wonderful goal to strive for throughout our lives. We are fortunate to have a Bible full of stories of men and women who played a role in God's plan for salvation. By studying their stories, we can better understand our own journey of faith and the path to Heaven.

D. Review Student Textbook Activity Page (10 minutes)

Note Alternative Option: Omit step D–1 if you choose to have the participants complete the activity page at home after the session.

1. Ask the participants to **turn to the activity** on page 7 in the student textbook. Ask them to **check** their completed work as you review the answers. See the introduction in this catechist's guide for suggestions on how to do this.

2. After checking the answers, **summarize** key aspects of salvation history by **presenting the following points:**

    ▶ The Bible shows God's plan to free us from sin and bring us to eternal life. Together, the events in the Bible that make up that plan are called salvation history.

    ▶ Salvation history can be broken down into eight different parts. In the Old Testament we have the first six: primeval history; patriarchs; Egypt and the Exodus; settling the Promised Land; kingdoms of Judah and Israel; and the Exile and return. The New Testament contains the final two parts: the life of Jesus Christ and the early Christian Church.

    ▶ The stories that reveal salvation history include men and women who showed great faith and sometimes great weakness. Yet all their stories witness to the unfailing love and mercy of God, who works through ordinary people to establish an everlasting relationship with each of us.

E. Integration Activity: The People of Salvation History (25 minutes)

In this activity the participants will explore the many individuals they will study during this course. The participants will only scratch the surface of one of the Bible people and then share what they have learned. By doing so, all the participants will get a taste of sessions to come.

1. **Ask** volunteers to share some of the interesting stories they heard from other participants during the Quick-Start Activity about favorite family trips or vacations. Then ask them to think about their own stories they shared. **Lead** a brief discussion, using the following questions as a guide:

    ▶ Why did you pick the story you did?

    ▶ Does your story reveal something about you or your family?

Then **continue** with these or similar words:

   ▶ Our family stories often reveal something about who we are and what we think is important. The same is true for the stories in the Bible. They say something about who we are as Christians and what we think is important. During our sessions together, we will explore the stories of many different people in our faith, so today we will take a quick look at each of the people we will study.

2. Give each participant a slip of paper cut from resource 1–A, "Bible People," with the names of their person and a Bible passage. Also give each participant a copy of handout 1–A, "Bible Person's Picture Frame." **Explain** that the participants will read the assigned Bible passage for their person. Then they will write the name of their person in the oval on the picture frame. On the three lines across the top of the picture, they will write three words that describe their person. In the middle of the picture frame, they will draw a picture of the scene described in their Bible passage.

3. After sufficient time **invite** the participants to share their work. Have them present the Bible people in the order they appear in the course. After each presentation ask the participants to tape their frames to a wall. By the end you will have a row of portraits that can be referred to frequently over the course of your sessions.

    Then **ask** the following questions:

    ▶ Whose story sounds the most interesting to you?

    ▶ Whose story do you know little about but are interested in learning more?

    Then refer to the wall of pictures and **conclude** with these or similar words:

    ▶ As our course progresses, we will learn a lot about each of these amazing people—their triumphs and their failures and how their stories help make up salvation history. Most important, we will learn of the amazing love God has for each of us and the lengths to which God will go to have a loving relationship with us.

    (*Note:* Leave the portraits up for the rest of the course if possible. If not, you may wish to set the appropriate picture on the prayer table for each lesson. You will need all the portraits during the final session.)

F. Announcements and Closing Prayer (5 minutes)

1. Make any needed **announcements. Assign** the background page to read and the activity to fill out for the next session if you will have the participants work on this at home.

2. Close by **leading** the participants in a short prayer, perhaps like the following:

    ▶ God, the story of your loving plan for us is amazing. Guide us as we learn about many of the wonderful people you chose to help you accomplish your plan of salvation for the world. May we learn from their stories so the story of salvation may become our own story. Amen.

Bible Person's Picture Frame

Bible People

Cut this resource into strips along the dotted lines. You will give each participant a Bible person to read about during step E, "Integration Activity: The People of Salvation History."

Adam and Eve	Genesis 3:21–23	Ezekiel	Ezekiel 37:1–14
Noah	Genesis 7:1–24	Ezra and Nehemiah	Ezra 7:6–10
Abraham and Sarah	Genesis 12:1–9	The Maccabees	1 Maccabees 2:15–26
Moses	Exodus 3:1–22	Mary of Nazareth	Luke 1:26–38
Joshua	Joshua 3:1–17	John the Baptist	Matthew 3:1–6
Samson	Judges 16:23–30	Jesus, the Christ	John 13:1–6
Ruth	Ruth 1:1–18	Peter	Matthew 16:13–19
King David	1 Samuel 17:41–50	Mary Magdalene	Matthew 28:1–10
King Solomon	1 Kings 3:1–12	Paul	Acts 16:16–30
Isaiah	Isaiah 6:1–8	Priscilla and Aquila	Acts 18:24–26

Resource 1–A: Permission to reproduce is granted. © 2010 by Saint Mary's Press.

Chapter 2

Introduction to the Old Testament

Session Focus

- The participants will learn key facts about the Old Testament:
    - It is also called the Hebrew Bible, and it tells the history of God's Covenant with the Chosen People.
    - It contains different types of writings, including history and poetry.
    - It can be broken down into four distinct sections.
    - Understanding the Old Testament is necessary if we wish to understand the New Testament.
- The participants will learn about the sections of the Old Testament:
    - They will find passages in the Old Testament.
    - They will note how the sections provide different types of information about God and our relationship with him.

At a Glance

A. Quick-Start Activity: Old Testament Images (5 minutes)
B. Opening Prayer Ritual (5 minutes)
C. Bible Story Sharing: The Lord's People (10 minutes)
D. Review Student Textbook Activity Page (10 minutes)
E. Integration Activity: Scripture Races (25 minutes)
F. Announcements and Closing Prayer (5 minutes)

Materials and Preparation

Materials Needed

For each participant:

❑ Bible and student textbook

❑ pencil

❑ handout 2–A, "Books of the Old Testament"

Additional materials:
- four sheets of easel-sized paper
- markers
- tape
- a simple prize for the winning teams during one of the activities

Other Preparation Steps

- Mark Sirach 2:10–11 in the Bible that will be used in the opening prayer ritual.
- Choose two students to process in with the Bible and a candle for the opening prayer ritual, providing directions as needed.
- Gather four sheets of easel-sized paper. Label them as follows:
  - Across the top of the first sheet: "The Pentateuch." Then list: Adam and Eve leave the garden; Noah builds an Ark; Moses delivers the Ten Commandments.
  - Across the top of the second sheet: "The Historical Books." Then list: Walls of Jericho fall; David defeats Goliath; King Solomon builds the Temple.
  - Across the top of the third sheet: "The Wisdom Books." Then list: Job's house collapses in a storm; People sing a psalm; Lady Wisdom calls out in the streets.
  - Across the top of the fourth sheet: "The Books of the Prophets." Then list: Isaiah advises kings; Ezekiel eats a scroll; Nehemiah helps rebuild the Temple.
- Make enough copies of handout 2–B, "Sections of the Old Testament." Cut the handout into strips so each participant can have four slips of paper with the four different sections of the Old Testament.

Background Reading

- Read the background page about the Old Testament on page 8 of the student textbook, including the suggested Bible passages.

Session Steps

A. Quick-Start Activity: Old Testament Images (5 minutes)

1. On the floor, place the markers, tape, and four sheets of easel-sized paper you prepared. Then **write** the following directions on the board:
   - Use markers to draw pictures on the easel-sized sheets of paper. Select the subject of the pictures from the list of Old Testament events on the sheet of paper you use.
2. As the students arrive, **instruct** them to follow the directions on the board.

B. Opening Prayer Ritual (5 minutes)

1. **Direct** the Bible bearer and candle bearer to take their places just outside the room or in the back of the room. **Gather** everyone else to stand around your prayer table. **Make** the Sign of the Cross and lead everyone in saying, "Let us remember that we are in the holy presence of God."

2. **Invite** the Bible bearer and candle bearer to silently process up to the prayer table and turn to face the group. The Bible bearer then **reads** the Scripture verse you have marked, Sirach 2:10–11. When finished, the reader says, "The Word of the Lord." Everyone responds, "Thanks be to God." The Bible bearer and candle bearer then place the Bible and candle on the prayer table and go to their places.

3. Invite everyone to sit down. **Introduce** the Old Testament in these or similar words:

    ▶ Today we will take a brief look at the Old Testament. The Old Testament is not "old" because it is out of date. Rather, it is called "old" because it tells about how God first began to plan for our salvation. The Old Testament tells how God called all people to obedience through God's Law and pointed toward the coming of Jesus Christ through the prophets. The Old Testament shows us God's amazing love and the roles different people have played in fulfilling his plan for salvation. That plan involved God's love and the people's response to that love through their own love and obedience, as we shall see in this passage.

C. Bible Story Sharing: The Lord's People (10 minutes)

Note Alternative Option: Omit step C if you choose to have the participants read the background sheet in the student textbook during class. Instead, the participants would use the time to complete the reading. You may wish to use the methods outlined in Suggestions for Reading Together, in the introduction to this catechist guide.

1. **Direct** the participants to open their Bibles to Deuteronomy 7:7–11. Provide help as needed but encourage the participants to find the passage on their own. **Read** the passage together. See the introduction in this catechist guide for different ways to do this.

2. **Lead** the group in a short reflection on the Bible passage. The following questions can help prompt discussion. Encourage all the participants to share their thoughts.

    ▶ Why does God choose to help God's own people? *(Answer: Not because they are numerous or powerful but because God loves them and wants to keep the promise made to their ancestors long ago.)*

    ▶ If you were one of the Israelites listening to Moses saying all this about God, how would you feel about your relationship with God?

▶ In what areas of life do most young people love and obey God? What areas do they most often need to work on?

3. **Summarize** the meaning of the Bible passage in these or similar words:

▶ Throughout the Old Testament, we read stories that show God's desire and unfolding plan for a loving relationship with God's own people. Sometimes the Israelites succeed in loving and obeying God, and sometimes they fail. But God's love and God's plan for our salvation never fails. As followers of Jesus, we too are called to love and obey God. We also have a mixture of success and failure, but we too can count on God's faithfulness no matter what.

D. Review Student Textbook Activity Page (10 minutes)

Note Alternative Option: Omit step D–1 if you choose to have the participants complete the activity page at home after the session.

1. Ask the participants to **turn to the activity** on page 9 in the student textbook. Ask them to **check** their completed work as you review the answers. See the introduction in this catechist guide for suggestions on how to do this.

2. After checking the answers, **summarize** key aspects of the Old Testament by **presenting the following points:**

▶ The Old Testament is also called the Hebrew Bible because it describes how God established a Covenant with the Chosen People.

▶ The Old Testament contains many different kinds of writings, like history, poetry, stories, sayings, and prophecies.

▶ There are four major sections within the Old Testament: the Pentateuch, the historical books, the wisdom books, and the books of the prophets.

▶ We need both the Old and the New Testaments to fully understand God's plan for us and how Jesus Christ fulfills that plan.

E. Integration Activity: Scripture Races (25 minutes)

In this activity the participants will consider their pictures of Old Testament stories and how they reflect the different sections found in the Old Testament.

Then they will participate in a group contest that will build their Bible skills and familiarity with the books and structure of the Old Testament.

1. Hang the four easel-sized sheets of paper on the wall. **Invite** volunteers to share what they drew on them during the Quick-Start Activity. Mention how each section gives us unique information about our faith.

Place the participants into groups of three or four. Tell them they will do Scripture races as teams. Distribute copies of handout 2–A, "Books of the Old Testament," and four slips of paper from handout 2–B, "Sections of the Old Testament." **Explain** that you will call out Old Testament Scripture passages, and the participants will look up the passages in their own Bibles. Once they find the passages, they will use handout 1–A to determine which section of the Bible the passage comes from. They will hold up the slip of paper with the name of that section on it. The team whose members all have their Bibles open to the correct passage and hold up the correct slip wins that round. **Encourage** team members to help one another. Then **ask:**

▶ Before we begin, can anyone explain how we look up passages in the Bible?

Help the participants understand how to use the book's name, chapter, and verse, and the Bible's table of contents, if need be, to look up a Scripture passage. Give one or two examples for practice. Encourage the team members to help one another when needed.

2. Then **begin** the team Scripture race. Call out any Old Testament passage by the name of the book, chapter, and verse (for example, Joshua 3:2). Determine which team wins based on the directions given above. After each round, ask the winning team to briefly explain what type of information it would expect to find in that particular section of the Old Testament. Keep score as you go and award the winning team a simple prize.

3. **Conclude** in these or similar words, referring again to the four sheets of easel-sized paper from earlier:

▶ Becoming familiar with the structure of the Old Testament and learning how to look up passages are important first steps in making the stories of the Bible part of your own faith lives. These pictures on the wall are just the tip of the iceberg when it comes to the amazing stories in the Old Testament. Yet what is truly amazing is how they all point to God's love and faithfulness.

F. Announcements and Closing Prayer (5 minutes)

1. Make any needed **announcements. Assign** the background page to read and the activity to fill out for the next session if you will have the participants work on this at home.

2. **Close** with prayer by asking all the participants to turn to Psalm 19:7–14. Say:

▶ The psalms are a form of prayer and often reflect on the Chosen People's relationship with God. So let us all pray Psalm 19:7–14 aloud together.

Read the psalm aloud together.

Books of the Old Testament

The Old Testament (Hebrew Bible)

(*Note:* Catholics use Bibles with forty-six books in the Old Testament. Protestants usually use Bibles with thirty-nine books in the Old Testament.)

Pentateuch
- Genesis
- Exodus
- Leviticus
- Numbers
- Deuteronomy

Historical Books
- Joshua
- Judges
- Ruth
- 1 and 2 Samuel
- 1 and 2 Kings
- 1 and 2 Chronicles
- Ezra
- Nehemiah
- Tobit*
- Judith*
- Esther
- 1 and 2 Maccabees*

Wisdom Books:
- Job
- Psalms
- Proverbs
- Ecclesiastes
- Song of Songs (Song of Solomon)
- Wisdom*
- Sirach*

Prophets
- Isaiah
- Jeremiah
- Lamentations
- Baruch*
- Ezekiel
- Daniel
- Hosea
- Joel
- Amos
- Obadiah
- Jonah
- Micah
- Nahum
- Habakkuk
- Zephaniah
- Haggai
- Zechariah
- Malachi

* This book is considered Deuterocanonical (meaning "second canon") and is not found in Protestant Bibles.

Handout 2–A: Permission to reproduce is granted. © 2010 by Saint Mary's Press.

Sections of the Old Testament

Copy this handout and then cut it out along the dotted lines. Make enough copies so each participant receives four slips of paper, each with one of the four sections of the Old Testament on it.

Pentateuch

Historical Books

Wisdom Books

Prophets

Pentateuch

Historical Books

Wisdom Books

Prophets

Handout 1–B: Permission to reproduce is granted. © 2010 by Saint Mary's Press.

Chapter 3

Adam and Eve

Session Focus

- The participants will learn key facts about Adam and Eve:
  - God creates Adam and Eve, the first human beings.
  - Before the Fall they live in perfect peace with God and each another.
  - They commit the first sin, called Original Sin.
  - They are banished from the garden as a result of their sin.
- The participants will study the story of Adam and Eve's covering themselves with fig leaves and reflect on key questions:
  - Why do young people sometimes cover up who they truly are, just as Adam and Eve did?
  - How can you find the strength simply to be the person God created?

At a Glance

A. Quick-Start Activity: Adam and Eve Picture Charades (5 minutes)
B. Opening Prayer Ritual (5 minutes)
C. Bible Story Sharing: Adam and Eve Eat from the Forbidden Fruit Tree (10 minutes)
D. Review Student Textbook Activity Page (10 minutes)
E. Integration Activity: Hiding Who We Are (25 minutes)
F. Announcements and Closing Prayer (5 minutes)

Materials and Preparation

Materials Needed

For each participant:
- ❏ Bible and student textbook
- ❏ pencil
- ❏ handout 3–A, "Fig Leaves"
- ❏ scissors

- ❏ markers
- ❏ glue

Additional materials:
- ❏ box
- ❏ magazines with pictures of a variety of people

Other Preparation Steps

- ❏ Mark Genesis 2:7 in the Bible that will be used in the opening prayer ritual.
- ❏ Choose two participants to process in with the Bible and a candle for the opening prayer ritual, providing directions as needed.
- ❏ Write the following on separate slips of paper:

  - God makes Adam from soil.
  - God creates Eve from Adam's rib.
  - Adam names the animals.
  - The snake tempts Eve.
  - Eve gives the apple to Adam.
  - Adam and Eve hide from God.
  - God makes clothes for Adam and Eve.
  - God kicks Adam and Eve out of the garden.

Background Reading

- Read the background page about Adam and Eve on page 10 of the student textbook, including the suggested Bible passages.
- If you are using *Breakthrough! The Bible for Young Catholics*, read the article "Original Sin," located near Genesis 3:1–24.

Session Steps

A. Quick-Start Activity: Adam and Eve Picture Charades (5 minutes)

1. **Set up** a game of picture charades for the participants to join as they arrive. Put the slips of paper you prepared in a box near the board. **Write** the following on the board:

   - Play a game of picture charades. One person at a time will pull a slip of paper from the box. Each slip has an event from the Book of Genesis. The person will draw a picture of the event on the board. Everyone else will guess the name of the event. The person who guesses correctly first will pull out the next slip and be the next person to draw.

2. As the participants arrive, **instruct** them to follow the directions on the board.

B. Opening Prayer Ritual (5 minutes)

1. **Direct** the Bible bearer and candle bearer to take their places just outside the room or in the back of the room. **Gather** everyone else to stand around your prayer table. **Make** the Sign of the Cross and lead everyone in saying, "Let us remember that we are in the holy presence of God."

2. **Invite** the Bible bearer and candle bearer to silently process up to the prayer table and turn to face the group. The Bible bearer then **reads** the Scripture verse you have marked, Genesis 2:7. When finished, the reader says, "The Word of the Lord." Everyone responds, "Thanks be to God." The Bible bearer and candle bearer then place the Bible and candle on the prayer table and go to their places.

3. Invite everyone to sit down. **Introduce** Adam and Eve in these or similar words:

   ▶ Today we will study Adam and Eve, the first man and woman God created. These two live in paradise. They can simply walk and talk with God. They can relax in the beautiful garden. Unfortunately, their desire for even more leads to serious consequences for them and all humanity. The problem begins when they make a bad choice, as we shall see in this passage.

C. Bible Story Sharing: Adam and Eve Eat from the Forbidden Fruit Tree (10 minutes)

Note Alternative Option: Omit step C if you choose to have the participants read the background sheet in the student textbook during class. Instead, the participants would use the time to complete the reading. You may wish to use the methods outlined in Suggestions for Reading Together, in the introduction to this catechist guide.

1. **Direct** the participants to open their Bibles to Genesis 3:1–7. Provide help as needed but encourage the participants to try to find the passage on their own. **Read** the passage together. See the introduction in this catechist guide for different ways to do this.

2. **Lead** the group in a short reflection on the Bible passage. Encourage all the participants to share their thoughts.

   ▶ What rule does God give Adam and Eve that the serpent wants them to break? *(Answer: They cannot eat or even touch the fruit of the tree in the middle of the garden.)*

   ▶ If you were Eve, what would you have said to the serpent? Why?

▶ Why is it difficult sometimes to do the right thing? What could help you in those situations?

3. **Summarize** the meaning of this Bible passage in these or similar words. (If you are using *Breakthrough! The Bible for Young Catholics*, consider reading to the group the article "Original Sin," located near this story):

> ▶ Adam and Eve live peacefully in the garden until the serpent tries to convince them they should have more. The serpent lies about God and causes Adam and Eve to question their trust in God. Unfortunately, by giving in to temptation and disobeying God, Adam and Eve commit the first sin, called Original Sin. We all face temptations. Like Eve, our peers may sometimes encourage us to do the wrong thing. In fact, Adam and Eve represent all of humanity in this story. We can learn from Adam and Eve's mistake and simply do what we know God is calling us to do.

D. Review Student Textbook Activity Page (10 minutes)

Note Alternative Option: Omit step D–1 if you choose to have the students complete the activity page at home after the session.

1. Ask the participants to **turn to the activity** on page 11 in the student textbook. Ask them to **check** their completed work as you review the answers. See the introduction in this catechist guide for suggestions to do this.

2. After checking the answers, **summarize** key aspects of Adam and Eve's lives by **presenting the following points:**

   ▶ The story of Adam and Eve reveals that God created the first man and woman in his own image.

   ▶ In the beginning Adam and Eve live in peace with God, nature, and each other in the garden.

   ▶ Adam and Eve commit the first sin, called Original Sin, when they choose to disobey God's command not to eat fruit from the tree in the middle of the garden.

   ▶ God punishes Adam and Eve by forcing them to leave the garden, but not before promising that someday Eve's offspring will defeat the snake and restore human kind's relationship with God. The snake represents evil, and the descendant of Eve who will later defeat evil is Jesus Christ. Jesus sacrifices himself to remove the sins of the world.

E. Integration Activity: Hiding Who We Are (25 minutes)

In this activity the participants will reflect on Adam and Eve's attempt to cover themselves after eating the forbidden fruit. The participants will consider ways young people try to cover up or hide who they are. Finally they will reflect on how we are called to accept ourselves the way God made us and openly accept others as well.

1. **Explain** that the participants have already examined the first part of the story about Adam and Eve's eating the fruit, so now they will see what happens to them after they eat the fruit. **Read** aloud Genesis 3:6–10. Then make the following points in these or similar words:

   ▶ Adam and Eve's downfall comes when they decide they are not fully happy with the way God made them and so choose to "become wise."

   ▶ Many of us are often like Adam and Eve when we think, "I am not pretty enough," "I am not tall enough," or "I am not smart enough."

   ▶ Like Adam and Eve, we are sometimes ashamed of who we truly are and try to hide our true selves. We might try to hang out with the "cool" crowd or participate in activities we do not like. To fit in, we may avoid activities we really like. We are not so different from Adam and Eve, who use fig leaves to cover up.

2. Make magazines available with pictures of different people in them. Distribute handout 3–A, "Fig Leaves." **Instruct** the participants to cut out the fig leaf and then to look for pictures in the magazines that represent ways people their age try to cover up who they truly are. Tell them to draw, write, or paste pictures onto the leaves that represent ways young people try to hide who they really are.

3. After sufficient time, **invite** volunteers to share what they have put on their fig leaves. Then **lead** a discussion using these or similar questions:

   ▶ Why do people choose "fig leaves" over letting others see who they really are?

   ▶ Can you tell the difference when people are being who they truly are versus trying to cover themselves up? How?

   ▶ What gives people the strength to be the selves that God created them to be?

   ▶ What might the world be like if all people accepted the way God made them?

   Then **conclude** with these or similar words:

   ▶ The story tells us that God created Adam and Eve, yet they were ashamed of who they were and tried to cover up. We too are created by God, just as Adam and Eve, and unfortunately we too sometimes try to cover up who we truly are. By remembering we are created in God's own image, we can find the strength to accept ourselves. We can also accept others when we remember they were created in God's image.

F. Announcements and Closing Prayer (5 minutes)

1. Make any needed **announcements. Assign** the background page to read and the activity to fill out for the next session if you will have the participants work on this at home.

2. Close by **leading** the participants in a short prayer, perhaps like the following one:

   ▶ God, help us learn from Adam and Eve's mistake. Give us the courage to allow the world to see us as you intended and help us to lovingly accept ourselves and others. Amen.

Fig Leaves

Cut out this fig leaf and then draw, write, or paste magazine pictures onto it that represent ways young people try to hide who they really are.

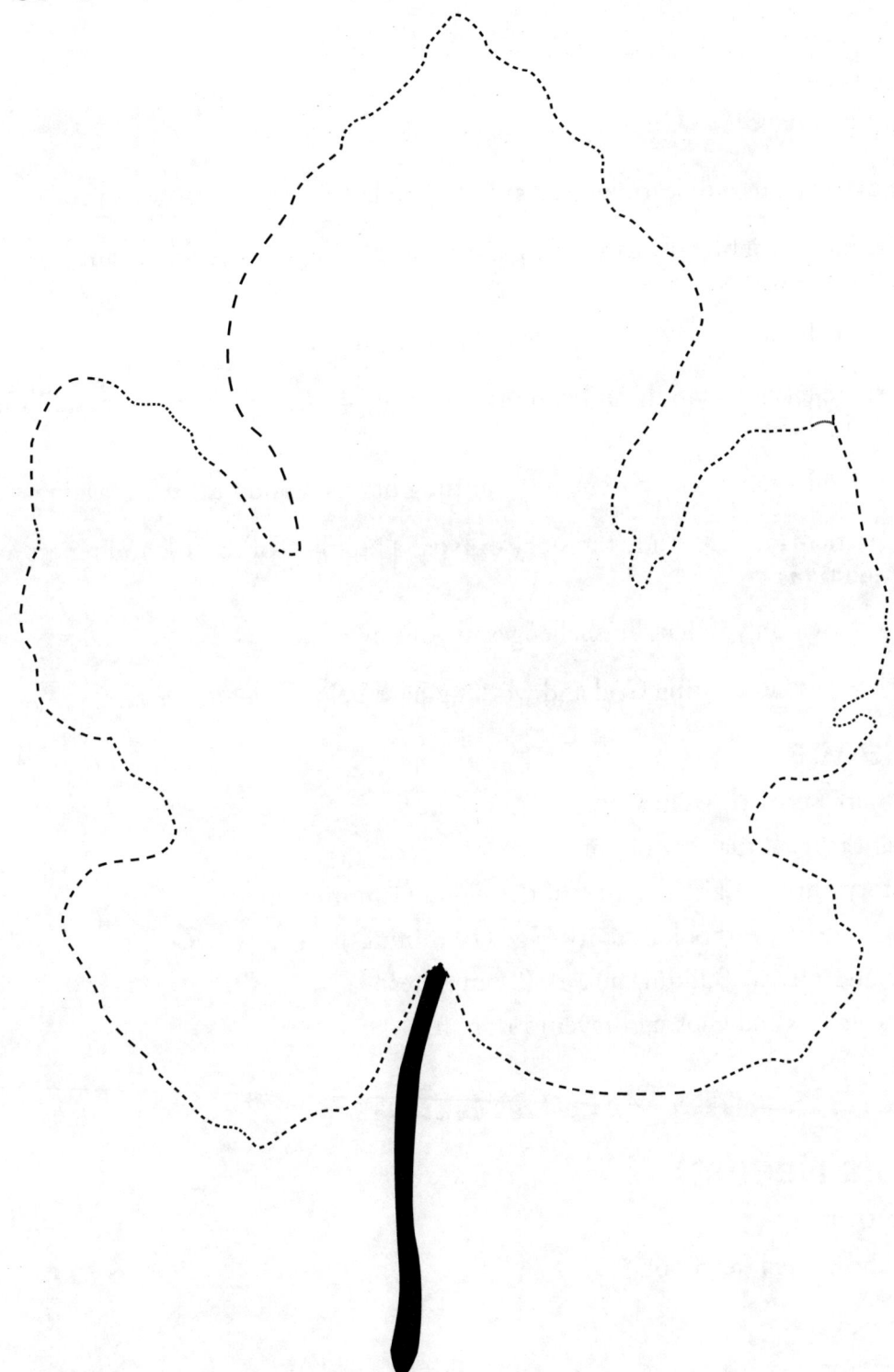

(This handout is from the *Teaching Activities Manual for "Breakthrough! The Bible for Young Catholics"* [Winona, MN: Saint Mary's Press, 2007], page 23. © 2007 by Saint Mary's Press. All rights reserved.)

Handout 3–A: Permission to reproduce is granted. © 2010 by Saint Mary's Press.

Chapter 4

Noah

Session Focus

- The participants will learn key facts about Noah:
  - He is a righteous man during a time when the world is filled with unrighteous people.
  - He builds an ark in response to God's command.
  - He takes his family and two of every animal into the ark, and they all survive the Flood.
  - God establishes a covenant, promising never to flood the earth again.
- The participants will study the story of Noah's building of the ark and reflect on key questions:
  - How can you handle challenges in your own life?
  - How can trusting God and working hard help you handle stress?

At a Glance

A. Quick-Start Activity: Animals for the Ark (5 minutes)
B. Opening Prayer Ritual (5 minutes)
C. Bible Story Sharing: The Coming of the Flood (10 minutes)
D. Review Student Textbook Activity Page (10 minutes)
E. Integration Activity: Building an Ark (25 minutes)
F. Announcements and Closing Prayer (5 minutes)

Materials and Preparation

Materials Needed

For each participant:
- ❏ Bible and student textbook
- ❏ pencil
- ❏ clay

For each small group:

- ❏ various materials to build a model ark: frozen-treat sticks, toothpicks, glue, paperclips, and so on

Additional materials:

- ❏ large, clear bowl to test-float arks
- ❏ pitcher of water

Other Preparation Steps

- ❏ Mark Genesis 6:5–8 in the Bible that will be used in the opening prayer ritual.
- ❏ Choose two participants to process in with the Bible and a candle for the opening prayer ritual, providing directions as needed.

Background Reading

- Read the background page about Noah on page 12 of the student textbook, including the suggested Bible passages.
- If you are using *Breakthrough! The Bible for Young Catholics*, read the article "God's Bright Spot," located near Genesis 6:1–12.

Session Steps

A. Quick-Start Activity: Animals for the Ark (5 minutes)

1. Put out enough clay for each participant to make a few small animals. **Write** the following on the board:

    ▶ Using the clay, make two of "every kind of animal" that walks on the earth. Make them only about one inch tall.

2. As the students arrive, **instruct** them to follow the directions on the board.

B. Opening Prayer Ritual (5 minutes)

1. **Direct** the Bible bearer and candle bearer to take their places just outside the room or in the back of the room. **Gather** everyone else to stand around your prayer table. **Make** the Sign of the Cross and lead everyone in saying, "Let us remember that we are in the holy presence of God."

2. **Invite** the Bible bearer and candle bearer to silently process up to the prayer table and turn to face the group. The Bible bearer then **reads** the Scripture verse you have marked,

Genesis 6:5–8. When finished, the reader says, "The Word of the Lord." Everyone responds, "Thanks be to God." The Bible bearer and candle bearer then place the Bible and candle on the prayer table and go to their places.

3. Invite everyone to sit down. **Introduce** Noah in these or similar words:

   ▶ Today we will study the story of Noah, the man best known for building an ark. But perhaps it is his strength of character that is most interesting. Noah stands out in the crowd simply because he is good. He is willing to do what is right even though nobody else is, as we shall see in this passage.

C. Bible Story Sharing: The Coming of the Flood (10 minutes)

Note Alternative Option: Omit step C if you choose to have the participants read the background sheet in the student textbook during class. Instead, the participants would use the time to complete the reading. You may wish to use the methods outlined in Suggestions for Reading Together, in the introduction to this catechist guide.

1. **Direct** the participants to open their Bibles to Genesis 7:1–24. Provide help as needed but encourage the participants to find the passage on their own. **Read** the passage together. See the introduction in this catechist guide for different ways to do this.

2. **Lead** the group in a short reflection on the Bible passage. If you are using *Breakthrough! The Bible for Young Catholics*, consider reading to the group the article "God's Bright Spot," located near this story. The following questions can help prompt discussion. Encourage all the participants to share their thoughts.

   ▶ How is Noah different from every other person living at the time? *(Answer: He is the only one who is doing what is right. All others, except his family, die in the Flood.)*

   ▶ If you were Noah, how might you feel being the only good person in the world and then knowing everybody else has died?

   ▶ Have you ever felt you were the only person trying to do the right thing? What gave you the courage to do the right thing?

3. **Summarize** the meaning of this Bible passage in these or similar words:

   ▶ Noah is a righteous man who follows his conscience, even though he is surrounded by people who do not do the right thing. Because of this, God chooses him to save humanity and all creation from the Flood. There are times we may feel we are the only ones trying to do the right thing. We must be brave like Noah. Just as Noah surrounds himself with his family, we must surround ourselves with people who will support us in our good decisions.

D. Review Student Textbook Activity Page (10 minutes)

Note Alternative Option: Omit step D–1 if you choose to have the participants complete the activity page at home after the session.

1. Ask the participants to **turn to the activity** on page 13 in the student textbook. Ask them to **check** their completed work as you review the answers. See the introduction in this catechist guide for suggestions on how to do this.

2. After checking the answers, **summarize** key aspects of Noah's story by **presenting the following points:**

    ▶ God sees that all the people except Noah have turned away from him and toward sin.

    ▶ God decides to flood the earth to destroy all living creatures but chooses to save Noah and his family because of their goodness.

    ▶ God asks Noah to build an ark. The ark saves Noah, his family, and two of each living creature from the Flood. By saving Noah and his family, God prevents the end of humankind.

    ▶ After the Flood, God makes a covenant, or solemn agreement, with Noah that God will never again use floods to destroy the earth. God puts up the rainbow as a sign and reminder of this promise.

E. Integration Activity: Building an Ark (25 minutes)

In this activity the participants will place themselves in Noah's shoes and attempt to build an ark to see if it floats. Although Noah faces an enormous challenge, he works hard and shows faith in completing it. The participants will consider ways they handle challenges and stress, and they will also consider how Noah can be an example to them in those situations.

1. **Place** the participants into groups of four or five. Then **say** something like the following:

    ▶ Today in your groups, you will be Noah. So listen carefully to what God tells Noah.

    Read aloud Genesis 6:14–16. Then continue:

    ▶ Just as Noah built an ark and received specific dimensions from God, you too are to build an ark. Your group must build one that is four inches by six inches.

2. **Give** each group supplies to build their arks. Once they have completed construction, pull out a large, clear bowl and a pitcher of water. **Read** aloud Genesis 7:11–12. Then pour the water into the bowl and **read** aloud Genesis 7:13–14. Then say these or similar words:

> ▶ The rains have come and the animals are ready. It is time to test out your arks. Each group will come forward to see if its ark floats. If it floats we will begin adding the animals you made during the Quick-Start Activity until it cannot hold any more.
>
> **Invite** the groups to come forward to test their arks.

3. After the groups have tried floating their arks, **lead** a discussion using the following questions as a guide:

   > ▶ What was the most difficult part about building the ark?
   >
   > ▶ Before you put your ark in the water, were you sure it would float? Do you think Noah felt any stress about taking on the challenge of building the ark? How do you think he might have handled the stress of knowing that the fate of the world was in his hands?
   >
   > ▶ How do you handle stress in your daily life?
   >
   > ▶ How might Noah's faith and hard work be an example to us when we are in stressful situations?

4. Then **conclude** with these or similar words:

   > ▶ Noah is given an enormous task—to save not only himself but also the existence of humankind from the Flood. Imagine the amount of stress Noah faces. Each board, each stroke of his hammer has to be just right or risk the ability of the ark to float. One man alone would have a difficult time under that pressure. Fortunately for Noah he is not alone. God is on his side. By working hard and trusting in God, Noah fulfills God's command and successfully saves himself and the existence of humankind. When we are faced with overwhelming challenges, or even small ones, we can be like Noah by working hard and trusting God.

F. Announcements and Closing Prayer (5 minutes)

1. Make any needed **announcements. Assign** the background page to read and the activity to fill out for the next session if you will have the participants work on this at home.

2. Close by **leading** the participants in **a short prayer,** perhaps like the following:

   > ▶ God, when we are faced with challenges, help us trust you and seek the support of those who love us. Amen.

Chapter 5

Abraham and Sarah

Session Focus

- The participants will learn key facts about Abraham and Sarah:
  - Abraham and Sarah faithfully follow God.
  - God forms a covenant with them and promises to make their descendants as numerous as the stars.
  - God gives them a son despite their old age.
  - God tests Abraham by asking him to sacrifice his son, Isaac.
- Participants will study the story of how God changed Abraham's and Sarah's names from Abram and Sarai and reflect on key questions:
  - What do Abram's and Sarai's new names mean and why does God change them?
  - How can you work with God to make the world a more loving place?

At a Glance

A. Quick-Start Activity: What Describes Me Best? (5 minutes)
B. Opening Prayer Ritual (5 minutes)
C. Bible Story Sharing: God Makes a Covenant with Abraham (10 minutes)
D. Review Student Textbook Activity Page (10 minutes)
E. Integration Activity: My Name and God's Plan (25 minutes)
F. Announcements and Closing Prayer (5 minutes)

Preparation and Materials

Materials Needed

For each participant:
- ❏ Bible and student textbook
- ❏ pencil
- ❏ paper

Additional materials:

- ❏ index cards, enough to write the meaning of each participant's name

Other Preparation Steps

- ❏ Mark Genesis 17:1–2 in the Bible that will be used in the opening prayer ritual.
- ❏ Choose two participants to process in with the Bible and a candle for the opening prayer ritual, providing directions as needed.
- ❏ Research the meaning of each of your participants' first names. For each name, write only its meaning on an index card, but do not write the name. Keep a master list with the names and meanings for yourself. (Because some names may come from family names or names of places and do not have descriptive meanings, consider adding a few extra names and their meanings to your list and simply explain this to the participants when you reveal all the names.)

Background Reading

- Read the background page about Abraham and Sarah on page 14 of the student textbook, including the suggested Bible passages.

Session Steps

A. Quick-Start Activity: What Describes Me Best? (5 minutes)

1. On a table, put the index cards with the meanings of your participants' names on them. **Write** the following on the board:

    ▶ Find the card in the pile that you think best describes you. Hold on to the card for later in the session.

2. As the participants arrive, **instruct** them to follow the directions on the board.

B. Opening Prayer Ritual (5 minutes)

1. **Direct** the Bible bearer and candle bearer to take their places just outside the room or in the back of the room. **Gather** everyone else to stand around your prayer table. **Make** the Sign of the Cross and lead everyone in saying, "Let us remember that we are in the holy presence of God."

2. **Invite** the Bible bearer and candle bearer to silently process up to the prayer table and turn to face the group. The Bible bearer then **reads** the Scripture verse you have marked, Genesis 17:1–2. When finished, the reader says, "The Word of the Lord." Everyone responds, "Thanks be to God." The Bible bearer and candle bearer then place the Bible and candle on the prayer table and go to their places.

3. Invite everyone to sit down. **Introduce** Abraham and Sarah in these or similar words:

> ▶ Today we will study Abraham and Sarah, a couple whom God calls to a new land to fulfill a wonderful plan. Abraham willingly enters into a relationship with God. In the relationship Abraham agrees to obey God. Evidence of both Abraham's and Sarah's obedience to God's will is shown by their great trust in God, as we shall see in this Bible story.

C. Bible Story Sharing: God Makes a Covenant with Abraham (10 minutes)

Note Alternative Option: Omit step C if you choose to have the participants read the background sheet in the student textbook during class. Instead, the participants would use the time to complete the reading. You may wish to use the methods outlined in Suggestions for Reading Together, in the introduction to this catechist guide.

1. **Direct** the participants to open their Bibles to Genesis 15:1–21. Provide help as needed but encourage the participants to find the passage on their own. **Read** the passage together. See the introduction in this catechist guide for different ways to do this.

2. **Lead** the group in a short reflection on the Bible passage. The following questions can help prompt discussion. Encourage all the participants to share their thoughts.

> ▶ What does God promise Abram? *(Answer: God promises Abram an heir, countless descendants, and vast amounts of land.)*

> ▶ Knowing there was no light pollution at the time, imagine how many stars must have been visible during the night. How do you think Abram, a man with no children, felt looking up at the sky and hearing God say his descendants would be as numerous as the stars?

> ▶ Name some ways young people can show their trust in God.

3. **Summarize** the meaning of this Bible passage in these or similar words:

> ▶ Abraham and Sarah are old and childless when God appears and promises to give Abraham countless descendants. What seems impossible at the time turns out to be another opportunity for Abraham to show great trust in God and for God to show his faithfulness to his word. Often we are challenged to simply trust God, yet it can be difficult. We can remember Abraham and how his trust is rewarded beyond his wildest dreams.

D. Review Student Textbook Activity Page (10 minutes)

Note Alternative Option: Omit step D–1 if you choose to have the participants complete the activity page at home after the session.

1. Ask the participants to **turn to the activity** on page 15 in the student textbook. Ask them to **check** their completed work as you review the answers. See the introduction in this catechist guide for suggestions on how to do this.

2. After checking the answers, **summarize** key aspects of Abraham's and Sarah's lives by **presenting the following points:**

    ▶ God calls Abram and Sarai to move to a new land, and he changes their names to Abraham and Sarah.

    ▶ God and Abraham enter into a covenant in which God promises to make Abraham's descendants as numerous as the stars. Abraham promises to be faithful to God alone.

    ▶ Although they are old, Abraham and Sarah conceive, and Sarah bears their only son, Isaac.

    ▶ God asks Abraham to sacrifice Isaac. Abraham begins to do as God asks, but God sees Abraham's faithfulness and stops him. Abraham is rewarded for his trust in God.

E. Integration Activity: My Name and God's Plan (25 minutes)

In this activity the participants will consider certain phrases or characteristics they think describe themselves. Then they will explore the meaning of Abraham's and Sarah's names and why God changes them. The participants will reflect on their own names and relate their meanings to the participants' calling to follow God and change the world for the better.

1. **Invite** volunteers to share the card they selected for themselves during the Quick-Start Activity. Ask them to explain why they picked that particular card. Then **say** these or similar words:

    ▶ Each of you picked a card because you felt it said something about you. The interesting thing about names is that each person's name also has a meaning and can sometimes say something about that person. In fact, the descriptions you picked out are actually from the meanings of the names of each of us.

    Then **reveal** the names with the meanings by reading your master list.

2. Then **say** these or similar words:

    ▶ Many names in the Bible also have meanings. *Peter* means "rock" and *Jesus* in Hebrew means "God is salvation." Abraham's name means "father of a multitude," and Sarah's name means "princess or queen." Listen to how Abraham and Sarah got their names:

Read Genesis 17:1–6,15–16. Then ask:

> ▶ Why does God change their names? *(Answer: So their names will reflect the lives they are called to live as a result of their Covenant relationship with God.)*

3. **Give** each participant a sheet of paper and a pencil and then say:

> ▶ Abraham's and Sarah's willingness to have a relationship with God and follow God's plan for them has helped change the world. Their faithfulness helped found Judaism and, as a result, Christianity. Like Abraham and Sarah, God has a plan for each of us to change the world for the better in some way. Take a moment to think about the meaning of your own name. Then on a sheet of paper write your name and its meaning. Underneath write ways the unique meaning of your name can be connected with ways you can work with God to help change the world for the better.

Invite the participants to share what they have written.

4. Then **conclude** with these or similar words:

> ▶ As Abraham and Sarah's story reminds us, when we work with God, nothing is impossible. They begin as two childless nomads and end up with descendants as numerous as the stars, some of them kings. God has a plan for each of us to make the world a better, more loving place. We can try to follow God's plan and imagine what wonderful things God has in store for us.

Announcements and Closing Prayer (5 minutes)

1. Make any needed **announcements. Assign** the background page to read and the activity to fill out for the next session if you will have the participants work on this at home.

2. Close by **leading** the participants in a short prayer, perhaps like the following:

> ▶ Let us simply show our desire to follow God as Abraham did by praying the words Jesus taught us.

Lead everyone in praying the Lord's Prayer.

Chapter 6

Moses

Session Focus

- The participants will learn key facts about Moses:
  - By means of the burning bush, God calls him to lead the Israelites to freedom.
  - Moses bravely goes to the Pharaoh and requests the Israelites' freedom.
  - He is a great leader during difficult times when the Israelites wander through the desert.
  - He receives the Ten Commandments from God.
- The participants will study the story of the Israelites' crossing of the Red Sea and reflect on key questions:
  - What frightening or worrisome situations do young people face today?
  - What can you learn from Moses' command to the Israelites to be still and let God take charge?

At a Glance

A. Quick-Start Activity: Drawing Out Worries (5 minutes)
B. Opening Prayer Ritual (5 minutes)
C. Bible Story Sharing: God Calls Moses (10 minutes)
D. Review Student Textbook Activity Page (10 minutes)
E. Integration Activity: Parting the Red Sea (25 minutes)
F. Announcements and Closing Prayer (5 minutes)

Preparation and Materials

Materials Needed

For each participant:
- ❏ Bible and student textbook
- ❏ pencil
- ❏ straw
- ❏ slip of paper

Additional materials:

- ❏ 9-by-13-inch pan
- ❏ water to fill the pan ½-inch deep
- ❏ 13-inch strip of masking tape with the words *Path to Freedom* written on it in waterproof ink

Other Preparation Steps

- ❏ Mark Philippians 4:6 in the Bible that will be used in the opening prayer ritual.
- ❏ Choose two participants to process in with the Bible and a candle for the opening prayer ritual, providing directions as needed.
- ❏ Along the bottom of the 9-by-13-inch pan, center the 13-inch piece of masking tape with the words *Path to Freedom*. Add water until it is about ½-inch deep.

Background Reading

- Read the background page about Moses on page 16 of the student textbook, including the suggested Bible passages.
- If you are using *Breakthrough! The Bible for Young Catholics,* read the article "Remember Who's in Charge," located near Exodus 14:10–14.

Session Steps

A. Quick-Start Activity: Drawing Out Fear (5 minutes)

1. **Write** the following on the board:

    ▶ Draw pictures on the board of things people worry about. Below your picture write the name of the worry.

2. As the students arrive, **instruct** them to follow the directions on the board.

B. Opening Prayer Ritual (5 minutes)

1. **Direct** the Bible bearer and candle bearer to take their places just outside the room or in the back of the room. **Gather** everyone else to stand around your prayer table. **Make** the Sign of the Cross and lead everyone in saying, "Let us remember that we are in the holy presence of God."

2. **Invite** the Bible bearer and candle bearer to silently process up to the prayer table and turn to face the group. The Bible bearer then **reads** the Scripture verse you have marked, Philippians 4:6. When finished, the reader says, "The Word of the Lord." Everyone responds, "Thanks be to God." The Bible bearer and candle bearer then place the Bible and candle on prayer table and go to their places.

3. Invite everyone to sit down. **Introduce** Moses in these or similar words:

   ▶ Today we will study Moses, a man with humble beginnings who becomes a great leader. During his life Moses has many adventures. He meets God in the form of a burning bush, he leads the Israelites through the Red Sea, and he receives the Ten Commandments directly from God. Yet this great man doubts himself and has to learn that despite his own weaknesses, God can still use him to do great deeds, as we shall see in this passage.

C. Bible Story Sharing: God Calls Moses (10 minutes)

Note Alternative Option: Omit step C if you choose to have the participants read the background sheet in the student textbook during class. Instead, the participants would use the time to complete the reading. You may wish to use the methods outlined in Suggestions for Reading Together, in the introduction to this catechist guide.

1. **Direct** the students to open their Bibles to Exodus 3:1–22. Provide help as needed but encourage the participants to find the passage on their own. **Read** the passage together. See the introduction in this catechist guide for different ways to do this.

2. **Lead** the group in a short reflection on the Bible passage. The following questions can help prompt discussion. Encourage all the participants to share their thoughts.

   ▶ When God speaks from the burning bush, where does God send Moses and why? *(Answer: God sends Moses to the king of Egypt so Moses can lead God's people out of Egypt to freedom.)*

   ▶ How do you think you would have responded to God if you were Moses?

   ▶ When Moses first hears God's plan to confront the king, Moses focuses on his own weakness and questions his own worthiness to do what God asks of him. Think about times when a poor self-image has prevented you from doing God's will. Can you name a time when you doubted yourself only to find out that you were able to do what you needed to do?

3. **Summarize** the meaning of this Bible passage in these or similar words:

   ▶ God is aware of the Israelites' suffering and decides it is time to free them from their enslavement. God chooses Moses to confront the king of Egypt and lead the Israelites. Moses openly reveals his doubts to God, and in return God reassures Moses he will not walk this difficult journey alone.

D. Review Student Textbook Activity Page (10 minutes)

Note Alternative Option: Omit step D–1 if you choose to have the participants complete the activity page at home after the session.

1. Ask the participants to **turn to the activity** on page 17 in the student textbook. Ask them to **check** their completed work as you review the answers. See the introduction in this catechist's guide for suggestions on how to do this.

2. After checking the answers, summarize key aspects of Moses' life by **presenting the following points:**

   ▶ God appears to Moses in the form of a burning bush and asks him to confront the king of Egypt and free the Israelites from slavery.

   ▶ God sends the plagues to convince Pharaoh to let the Israelites go. To escape the effects of the tenth plague, Moses leads the Israelites in the first Passover. In it, Moses instructs the Israelites to mark their doorposts with the blood of a lamb and to prepare a sacred meal.

   ▶ Moses leads the Israelites out of Egypt and through the Red Sea.

   ▶ Moses receives the Ten Commandments from God on Mount Sinai.

E. Integration Activity: Parting the Red Sea (25 minutes)

In this activity the participants will consider the fear the Israelites feel of being caught between charging chariots and the Red Sea. The participants will consider that Moses calls the Israelites to be still and let God be in charge of the situation. When young people are surrounded by worries, they too can be still and let God take charge.

1. Start by **telling** the participants the story of the crossing of the Red Sea, found in Exodus, chapter 14. The story is long, so summarize the beginning and then read aloud Exodus 14:10–27. Have the participants find the story in their own Bibles and follow along as you read.

2. After the reading, tell the participants they will have a chance to try to part the Red Sea for themselves. On a table put out the 9-by-13-inch pan with ½ inch of water and the 13-inch strip of masking tape down the middle with the words *Path to Freedom* written on it. Give each participant a straw and have the participants come up individually at first, then in groups, to part the sea by blowing the water off the path to freedom represented by the masking tape under the water. In the end see if everybody can blow at once to completely reveal the entire path.

3. Ask the participants to take their seats. Discuss briefly whether it was hard to part the sea. Then ask them to imagine being a slave and being offered freedom. As they leave, they are caught between soldiers in chariots coming to kill them on one side and not a half-inch of water but an entire sea of water blocking their way on the other side. Then ask the participants the following questions:

▶ How scared do you think the Israelites are at this point?

▶ What do you think is going through their minds? *(Answers may include death, loss of everything, family, broken promises, lost hopes.)*

▶ Knowing how the Israelites feel, Moses tells them to simply be still. How hard would it be to be still in a situation like that?

▶ Who do the Israelites think is in charge when they are trapped between the army and the sea? Who does Moses know is in charge?

4. In these or similar words, **talk** about trust in God when we are weighed down by fear or worry:

   ▶ The Israelites have been on an emotional roller coaster. They start as beaten-down slaves who are excited with Moses' plan for freedom. Then just when they are heading out of Egypt, they find themselves being hunted down by the king of Egypt and trapped by the sea. When all hope seems lost, Moses reminds the people that God is in charge, and the Red Sea miraculously opens up so they can walk away safe and sound.

   ▶ Life can often seem like a roller coaster. Things may be going well one day, and then it all seems to fall apart. We may not find ourselves chased by chariots, but we can find ourselves caught up with other kinds of worries like the ones you drew on the board earlier. *(Note: Specifically mention some of the worries written on the board.)* Just like Moses' directions to the Israelites, we too are called to be still and let God take charge of the situation. I now invite you to think about what you worry most about and how you can let God take charge of the situation.

5. After a minute, **give** each participant a slip of paper and a pencil. **Instruct** the participants to write on the slips the thing they worry most about. Tell them no one else will see their slips and direct them to fold the slips once and hold on to them for the closing prayer.

6. After allowing time for writing, **conclude** by saying the following. (If you are using *Breakthrough! The Bible for Young Catholics*, consider reading to the group the article "Remember Who's in Charge," located near this story.)

   ▶ When you are worried and scared and do not see a way out, remember to follow Moses' call to be still and let God take control.

F. Announcements and Closing Prayer (5 minutes)

1. Make any needed **announcements. Assign** the background page to read and the activity to fill out for the next session if you are having the participants work on this at home.

2. Close by **leading** the participants in a short prayer, perhaps like the following:

   ▶ God, we humbly lay our worries before you and ask that you give us the courage like Moses to be still and allow you to be in charge. Amen.

Then invite the participants to come forward and cast their folded slips in the "sea" (the pan with water) as a sign of their desire to let it go and let God take charge. Conclude by praying the Lord's Prayer together.

Chapter 7

Joshua

Session Focus

- The participants will learn key facts about Joshua:
    - He becomes the leader of the Israelites when Moses dies.
    - He leads the Israelites in the dramatic capture of Jericho.
    - He leads the Israelites into the Promised Land.
    - He shows steadfast faith in God's promise to take care of the Chosen People.
- The participants will study events from the life of Joshua and reflect on key questions:
    - Whom do you consider to be a hero and why?
    - How can you use Joshua as a model for measuring your own heroes?

At a Glance

A. Quick-Start Activity: Who Are Your Heroes? (5 minutes)
B. Opening Prayer Ritual (5 minutes)
C. Bible Story Sharing: Joshua and the Renewal of the Covenant (10 minutes)
D. Review Student Textbook Activity Page (10 minutes)
E. Integration Activity: A Hero in the News (25 minutes)
F. Announcements and Closing Prayer (5 minutes)

Preparation and Materials

Materials Needed

For each participant:
- ❏ Bible and student textbook
- ❏ pencil
- ❏ paper

Additional materials:
- ❏ props for news broadcast skits, possibly including sports coats, blazers, pretend microphones, and so on

Other Preparation Steps

❏ Mark Joshua 1:9 in the Bible that will be used in the opening prayer ritual.

❏ Choose two participants to process in with the Bible and a candle for the opening prayer ritual, providing directions as needed.

Background Reading

- Read the background page about Joshua on page 18 of the student textbook, including the suggested Bible passages.

- If you are using *Breakthrough! The Bible for Young Catholics*, read the article "Remembering God's Goodness," located near Joshua 24:1–15.

Session Steps

A. Quick-Start Activity: Who Are Your Heroes? (5 minutes)

1. **Write** the following on the board:
   ▶ Who are your heroes? On a sheet of paper define the word *hero*. Then write down the names of your heroes, male or female, and what makes each a hero.

2. As the participants arrive, give them a pencil and a sheet of paper and **instruct** them to follow the directions on the board.

B. Opening Prayer Ritual (5 minutes)

1. **Direct** the Bible bearer and candle bearer to take their places just outside the room or in the back of the room. **Gather** everyone else to stand around your prayer table. **Make** the Sign of the Cross and lead everyone in saying, "Let us remember that we are in the holy presence of God."

2. **Invite** the Bible bearer and candle bearer to silently process up to the prayer table and turn to face the group. The Bible bearer then **reads** the Scripture verse you have marked, Joshua 1:9. When finished, the reader says, "The Word of the Lord." Everyone responds, "Thanks be to God." The Bible bearer and candle bearer then place the Bible and candle on the prayer table and go to their places.

3. Invite everyone to sit down. **Introduce** Joshua in these or similar words:

   ▶ Today we will study Joshua, a heroic leader of the Israelites. He shows great trust in God's promise to take care of the Chosen People. Perhaps part of Joshua's great trust in God is his awareness of God's care for Israel in the past and how God has never let the people down. Joshua uses Israel's history to promote further trust in God, as we shall see in this passage.

C. Bible Story Sharing: Joshua and the Renewal of the Covenant (10 minutes)

Note Alternative Option: Omit step C if you choose to have the participants read the background sheet in the student textbook during class. Instead, the participants would use this time to complete the reading. You may wish to use the methods outlined in Suggestions for Reading Together, in the introduction to this catechist guide.

1. **Direct** the participants to open their Bibles to Joshua 24:1–15. Provide help as needed but encourage the participants to find the passage on their own. **Read** the passage together. See the introduction in this catechist guide for different ways to do this.

2. **Lead** the group in a short reflection on the Bible passage. If you are using *Breakthrough! The Bible for Young Catholics,* consider reading to the group the article "Remembering God's Goodness," located near this story. The following questions can help prompt discussion. Encourage all the participants to share their thoughts.

   ▶ After listing all the things God has done for the Israelites, what choice does Joshua give the Israelites, and what is Joshua's decision? *(Answer: They have to choose if they will continue to serve God or turn away and worship false gods. Joshua proclaims that he and his family will remain faithful and serve only God.)*

   ▶ If you were Joshua, what would you have said to the people if they had said they wanted to serve other gods instead?

   ▶ If you were like Joshua and were to list all the things God had done for you, what would be on your list? How would that list affect your desire to serve God?

3. **Summarize** the meaning of this Bible passage in these or similar words:

   ▶ The Israelites finally find their new home in the Promised Land. Joshua takes time with the Israelites and lists all the amazing things God has done for them since Moses saw the burning bush. What stands out in his list is the unfailing faithfulness, not of the people, but of God. God has kept every promise he has made, even when the people do not keep their end of the deal. We are like the Israelites—sometimes we remain faithful, and sometimes we fail. But if we seek to remember all the wonderful things God has done for us, as Joshua does, then our desire to do better and serve God more will grow.

D. Review Student Textbook Activity Page (10 minutes)

Note Alternative Option: Omit step D–1 if you choose to have the participants complete the activity page at home after the session.

1. Ask the participants to **turn to the activity** on page 19 in the student textbook. Ask them to **check** their completed work as you review the answers. See the introduction in this catechist guide for suggestions on how to do this.

2. After checking the answers, **summarize** key aspects of Joshua's life by **presenting the following points:**

   ▶ Joshua wants the Israelites to overcome their fears and trust God's protection as they seek to enter the Promised Land.

   ▶ Before Moses dies he appoints Joshua the next leader of Israel. Shortly after Moses' death, Joshua leads the Israelites through the River Jordan into the Promised Land.

   ▶ Joshua has constant faith in God. Following God's command, he leads the Israelites in an unusual way to defeat the people of Jericho by marching around the city and making the walls fall.

E. Integration Activity: A Hero in the News (25 minutes)

In this activity the participants will identify their own heroes. Then they will study the life of Joshua, a Bible hero, and present news broadcasts on important events from his life. The participants will then compare their own heroes to Joshua and consider what defines a true hero.

1. Refer the participants to their sheet of paper from the Quick-Start Activity. Then invite volunteers to **share** their definitions of the word *hero* and the names of their heroes. Ask them to explain what about those people makes them heroes.

   Then **say** these or similar words:

   ▶ As we have already seen, Joshua is a hero. The Bible records many stories of Joshua's heroism. Because many of our modern heroes end up on the evening news, we will be putting Joshua on the evening news today too. Your task will be to read a passage about Joshua and then develop an evening news broadcast about it.

2. **Place** the participants into three groups. Assign each group one of the following passages about Joshua's life:

   - Joshua 3:5,14–17 (Joshua leads the Israelites into the Promised Land.)
   - Joshua 6:1–4,15–16,20 (The walls of Jericho fall.)
   - Joshua 24:29–31 (The death of Joshua.)

   Tell the participants they will read their passage and then develop a news broadcast about it. Their broadcast should include a news anchor, a reporter on the scene, and witnesses for the reporter to interview. Provide the various props you have collected for their broadcasts.

3. After they have prepared their broadcasts, **invite** the groups to present them. Have them present in the same order the passages appear in the Bible to help the flow of Joshua's story over time.

   After the broadcasts, **lead** a discussion, using the following questions:

   ▶ How does Joshua compare to your definition of the word *hero* or to the heroes we mentioned earlier?

   ▶ How might the story of Joshua change your definition of *hero*?

4. Then **conclude** with these or similar words:

   ▶ Throughout his life Joshua shows heroic trust in God's promise to take care of Israel. Because of his trust in God, Joshua becomes a great leader for the Chosen People. Under Joshua's leadership the Israelites cross the Jordan River, see the walls of Jericho fall, and witness the defeat of those who try to prevent them from taking possession of the Promised Land. Joshua provides a great example of what it means to be a hero. We can learn to be careful about whom we consider a hero. Too often our society labels someone a hero who doesn't show true heroism, as Joshua does. We could be better people if our heroes were like Joshua: people who trust in God, do the right thing, and lead others to do the same.

F. Announcements and Closing Prayer (5 minutes)

1. Make any needed **announcements. Assign** the background page to read and the activity to fill out for next session if you will have the participants work on this at home.

2. Close by **leading** the participants in a short prayer, perhaps like the following:

   ▶ God, help us to be more like Joshua and always remember all the wonderful things you have done for us. May we live our lives simply trusting in all you have promised us. Amen.

Chapter 8

Samson

Session Focus

- The participants will learn key facts about Samson:

  - He is an Israelite leader whose life was dedicated to God from birth.

  - He is known for his incredible physical strength, as well as his weakness for getting angry and seeking revenge.

  - He marries a Philistine woman named Delilah, who betrays him, which leads to his death.

  - Despite his weaknesses, he turns to God in the end and defeats the Philistines.

- The participants will study the story of Samson and the woman from Timnah and reflect on key questions:

  - How do anger and revenge increase Samson's problems?

  - How can you better handle your own anger?

At a Glance

A. Quick-Start Activity: Riddles (5 minutes)
B. Opening Prayer Ritual (5 minutes)
C. Bible Story Sharing: An Angel Announces Samson's Birth to His Parents (10 minutes)
D. Review Student Workbook Activity Page (10 minutes)
E. Integration Activity: A Clay Story (25 minutes)
F. Announcements and Closing Prayer (5 minutes)

Preparation and Materials

Materials Needed

For each participant:
- ❏ Bible and student textbook
- ❏ pencil

For each small group:
- ❏ modeling clay

Other Preparation Steps

❏ Mark Judges 13:1–5 in the Bible that will be used in the opening prayer ritual.

❏ Choose two participants to process in with the Bible and a candle for the opening prayer ritual, providing directions as needed.

❏ Find two or three riddles your participants will find interesting. An Internet search can reveal sites with riddles.

Background Reading

- Read the background page about Samson on page 20 of the student textbook, including the suggested Bible passages.

- If you are using *Breakthrough! The Bible for Young Catholics,* read the article "Samson in Trouble," located near Judges 14:15—15:8.

Session Steps

A. Quick-Start Activity: Riddles (5 minutes)

1. **Write** a few riddles on the board, followed by this one:

   - Out of the eater came something to eat; out of the strong came something sweet.

2. As the participants arrive, **instruct** them to solve the riddles on the board.

B. Opening Prayer Ritual (5 minutes)

1. **Direct** the Bible bearer and candle bearer to take their places just outside the room or in the back of the room. **Gather** everyone else to stand around your prayer table. **Make** the Sign of the Cross and lead everyone in saying, "Let us remember that we are in the holy presence of God."

2. **Invite** the Bible bearer and candle bearer to silently process up to the prayer table and turn to face the group. The Bible bearer then **reads** the Scripture verses you have marked, Judges 13:1–5. When finished, the reader says, "The Word of the Lord." Everyone responds, "Thanks be to God." The Bible bearer and candle bearer then place the Bible and candle on the prayer table and go to their places.

3. Invite everyone to sit down. **Introduce** Samson in these or similar words:

   ▶ Today we will study Samson, a man known for his incredible physical strength. Yet having physical strength does not mean he always has the spiritual strength to do the right thing. Samson's temper and desire for revenge often lead him astray. Despite Samson's weaknesses, God has a plan for Samson. That plan begins right from Samson's birth, as we shall see in this passage.

C. Bible Story Sharing: An Angel Announces Samson's Birth to His Parents (10 minutes)

Note Alternative Option: Omit step C if you choose to have the participants read the background sheet in the student textbook during class. Instead, the participants would use the time to complete the reading. You may wish to use the methods outlined in Suggestions for Reading Together, in the introduction to this catechist guide.

1. **Direct** the participants to open their Bibles to Judges 13:1–24. Provide help as needed but encourage the participants to try to find the passage on their own. **Read** the passage together. See the introduction in this catechist guide for different ways to do this.

2. **Lead** the group in a short reflection on the Bible passage. The following questions can help prompt discussion. Encourage all the participants to share their thoughts.

   ▶ What question does Manoah, Samson's father, have for the angel? *(Answer: "What do we do with the boy once he is born?" or "What kind of life must he lead?")*

   ▶ If you were Samson, and your mom or dad told you about what the angel had said about you before you were born, what hopes or expectations would you have for yourself?

   ▶ What hopes or expectations do you have for yourself?

3. **Summarize** the meaning of this Bible passage in these or similar words:

   ▶ Samson's parents had been unable to have children, so imagine their joy at hearing the angel say a son is on the way. For most parents, finding out they are going to become mothers and fathers for the first time is both exciting and a little scary. Manoah's question about what to do once Samson arrives is the same question all parents have when they find out they are expecting. Just as Samson's parents ask about what type of life God wants their child to live, your parents may easily ask the same question about you. God has a plan for each of you. As with Samson, he has given you unique gifts and talents. Because you are getting older and making more decisions for yourself, you too can prayerfully ask God, "What kind of life am I to live?" and then work to live that life the best you can.

D. Review Student Textbook Activity Page (10 minutes)

Note Alternative Option: Omit step D–1 if you choose to have the participants complete the activity page at home after the session.

1. Ask the participants to **turn to the activity** on page 21 in the student textbook. Ask them to **check** their completed work as you review the answers. See the introduction in this catechist guide for suggestions on how to do this.

2. After checking the answers, **summarize** key aspects of Samson's life by **presenting the following points:**

   ▶ Samson's parents dedicate him to God at birth. Not cutting his hair, not drinking alcohol, and not touching dead bodies are signs of that commitment.

   ▶ Samson, who becomes a leader among the Israelites, is known for his incredible physical strength, even though spiritually he often fails.

   ▶ Samson marries a Philistine woman named Delilah, who betrays him by cutting his hair, which makes him lose his strength.

   ▶ In his final moments, Samson turns to God for strength and defeats the Philistines.

E. Integration Activity: A Clay Story (25 minutes)

In this activity the participants will use clay models to represent and consider how Samson handles his anger. They will reflect on the effect anger and revenge can have on problems and consider ways they can better handle their own anger and emotions.

1. **Invite** volunteers to answer the riddles you supplied for the Quick-Start Activity. Give them the correct answers to all but the last riddle. Then **say:**

   ▶ Samson liked riddles, so you can look for the answer to our final riddle in the story we will read.

   Place the participants into nine groups. **Give** each group modeling clay, and assign each group one of the following passages. (For small gatherings you may combine some of the passages or have the participants work individually.)

   - Judges 14:1–7
   - Judges 14:8–9
   - Judges 14:10–14
   - Judges 14:15–17
   - Judges 14:18–20
   - Judges 15:1–2
   - Judges 15:3–5
   - Judges 15:6
   - Judges 15:7–8

Instruct the groups to read Judges 14:1—15:8. They will then use the modeling clay to represent what is happening in their specific passages.

2. When the participants are finished making their clay representations, ask if anyone has found the answer to the final riddle. (If not, tell the participants the answer is a lion.) **Invite** each group to present its clay representation. Line up all the models to form a display of the entire story. Then **lead** a discussion, using these or similar questions:

   ▶ Why does Samson get angry? Does his anger solve the problem?

   ▶ How does getting even help or hurt Samson?

   ▶ How do you handle getting angry?

   ▶ What are some ways we can better handle our anger?

Conclude with these or similar words. (If you are using *Breakthrough! The Bible for Young Catholics,* consider reading aloud the article "Samson in Trouble," located near this story.)

   ▶ Samson is far from perfect. He often reacts to situations with little thought to what he is doing. As we see in the story, one poor reaction by Samson just leads to another, bigger problem. At the beginning of the passage, Samson is excited about getting married. By the end he is living in a cave all alone. As Samson's story shows, a series of bad choices can lead us where we originally had no intention of going—like from a wedding to a lonely cave. We can learn from Samson that it is wise to think before we act.

F. Announcements and Closing Prayer (5 minutes)

1. Make any needed **announcements. Assign** the background page to read and the activity to fill out for the next session if you will have the participants work on this at home.

2. Close by **inviting** the participants to shape the modeling clay from earlier into a new shape that symbolizes peace to them. Then lead them in a short prayer, perhaps like the following:

   ▶ God, you used your servant Samson despite his weakness for anger. We ask that you help us set aside our anger and seek peace. As a sign of our desire for peace, we offer these symbols. *(To the participants:)* I now invite each of you to place your peace symbol on our prayer table. Amen.

Lead everyone in praying the Lord's Prayer.

Chapter 9

Ruth

Session Focus

- The participants will learn key facts about Ruth:

  - Ruth is from Moab, an area with people who did not get along with the Israelites, but she had married an Israelite man who later died.

  - She chooses to leave Moab and go to Israel with her mother-in-law despite the challenges they will face.

  - She marries another Israelite and helps support her mother-in-law.

  - She is the great-grandmother of King David and an ancestor of Jesus.

- The participants will study the story of Ruth gathering grain in Boaz's field and reflect on key questions:

  - How do Ruth and Boaz choose to love others?

  - How might you be more like Ruth and Boaz?

At a Glance

A. Quick-Start Activity: Staying in Touch (5 minutes)
B. Opening Prayer Ritual (5 minutes)
C. Bible Story Sharing: Ruth's Generous Response to Naomi (10 minutes)
D. Review Student Textbook Activity Page (10 minutes)
E. Integration Activity: Text Messaging (25 minutes)
F. Announcements and Closing Prayer (5 minutes)

Preparation and Materials

Materials Needed

For each participant:
- ❏ Bible and student textbook

For each pair of participants:
- ❏ writing paper
- ❏ pencil

Additional materials:
- ❏ easel-sized paper or other large sheet of paper

❏ scissors, one pair

❏ crayons

Other Preparation Steps

❏ Mark Ruth 1:16 in the Bible that will be used in the opening prayer ritual.

❏ Choose two participants to process in with the Bible and a candle for the opening prayer ritual, providing directions as needed.

❏ On a large sheet of paper, draw a giant flip-open cell phone. On the LED screen (the top half of the phone), put an X and write *Cut this part out.* The drawing will be something like a puppet stage: the opening should be large enough so the participants' heads will fit through it as they stand behind it and read messages they will write.

Background Reading

- Read the background page about Ruth on page 22 of the student textbook, including the suggested Bible passages.

- If you are using *Breakthrough! The Bible for Young Catholics,* read the article "When Bad Things Happen," located near Ruth, chapter 1.

Session Steps

A. Quick-Start Activity: Staying in Touch (5 minutes)

1. Before the participants arrive, **place** on a table or floor the giant cell-phone drawing you have prepared. Place a pair of scissors and some crayons next to it. **Write** the following on the board:

   - Please help decorate our cell phone. Cut out only the one section labeled *Cut this part out.*

2. As the participants arrive, **instruct** them to follow the directions on the board.

B. Opening Prayer Ritual (5 minutes)

1. **Direct** the Bible bearer and candle bearer to take their places just outside the room or in the back of the room. **Gather** everyone else to stand around your prayer table. **Make** the Sign of the Cross and lead everyone in saying, "Let us remember that we are in the holy presence of God."

2. **Invite** the Bible bearer and candle bearer to silently process up to the prayer table and turn to face the group. The Bible bearer then **reads** the Scripture verse you have marked, Ruth 1:16. When finished, the reader says, "The Word of the Lord." Everyone responds, "Thanks be to God." The Bible bearer and candle bearer then place the Bible and candle on the prayer table and go to their places.

3. Invite everyone to sit down. **Introduce** Ruth in these or similar words:

   ▶ Today we will study Ruth, an unlikely hero in Israel's history, because she is from a group of people who do not like Israel. Yet through her loyalty, courage, and ability to love, she not only finds her way into Israel's history but also becomes the great-grandmother of King David and an ancestor of Jesus. Her story begins when she makes a difficult choice, as we shall see in this passage.

C. Bible Story Sharing: Ruth's Generous Response to Naomi (10 minutes)

Note Alternative Option: Omit step C if you choose to have the participants read the background sheet in the student textbook during class. Instead, the participants would use the time to complete the reading. You may wish to use the methods outlined in Suggestions for Reading Together, in the introduction to this catechist guide.

1. **Direct** the participants to open their Bibles to Ruth 1:6–18. Provide help as needed but encourage the participants to try to find the passage on their own. **Read** the passage together. See the introduction in this catechist guide for different ways to do this.

2. **Lead** the group in a short reflection on the Bible passage. If you are using *Breakthrough! The Bible for Young Catholics,* consider reading aloud the article "When Bad Things Happen," located near this story. The following questions can help prompt discussion. Encourage all the participants to share their thoughts.

   ▶ Why does Naomi tell her daughters-in-law to remain in Moab as she sets out to return to Judah? *(Answer: She wants them to return to their mothers in the hope that they will be well taken care of and possibly find new husbands to care for them.)*

   ▶ If you were one of Naomi's daughters-in-law, would you have returned home like Orpah or stayed with Naomi like Ruth?

   ▶ Ruth knows life will be difficult whether she stays in Moab or leaves with Naomi, but she chooses to face the difficult times with Naomi and God. Who has stood by you in tough times? How has this person supported you?

3. **Summarize** the meaning of this Bible passage in these or similar words.

   ▶ Naomi, Orpah, and Ruth have fallen on hard times. Without husbands or sons to take care of them, they will definitely be poor and could possibly even starve to death. Naomi makes the difficult choice to return to Judah and asks her daughters-in-law to return to their own families. Ruth's love for Naomi and for God, whom she most likely learned about from Naomi, prompts Ruth to pledge to stay by Naomi's side for life. When our loved ones face difficult times, we can show our love for them, and for God, by offering our support and care.

D. Review Student Textbook Activity Page (10 minutes)

Note Alternative Option: Omit step D–1 if you choose to have the participants complete the activity page at home after the session.

1. Ask the participants to **turn to the activity** on page 23 in the student textbook. Ask them to **check** their completed work as you review the answers. See the introduction in this catechist's guide for suggestions on how to do this.

2. After checking the answers, **summarize** key aspects of Ruth's life by **presenting the following points:**

   ▶ Ruth is from Moab, a region of people who were ancient enemies of Israel. Ruth had married an Israelite man who had left his homeland during a famine.

   ▶ Now a widow, Ruth leaves her own homeland to move to Judah with her mother-in-law, Naomi, who is also a widow.

   ▶ Ruth works hard to take care of Naomi. Ruth finally meets a man named Boaz, who marries her and takes good care of both Ruth and Naomi.

   ▶ Through her marriage to Boaz, Ruth has a son and is the great-grandmother of King David and an ancestor of Jesus.

E. Integration Activity: Text Messaging (25 minutes)

In this activity the participants will pretend to be Naomi and Ruth. They will read a Bible passage about Ruth gathering grain, then develop and present a text-message conversation that might have taken place between Naomi and Ruth during that day. The participants will then consider the kindness Boaz shows Ruth and ways they can imitate that kindness.

1. Refer to the cell phone the participants decorated during the Quick-Start Activity and **ask** them why so many people have cell phones. Mention the ways family members use them to stay in touch with one another, especially parents checking in with their children.

2. **Place** the participants in pairs. Give each pair a sheet of writing paper and a pencil. **Explain** that if Naomi had a cell phone, she surely would have wanted to check in with Ruth at times. Today in their pairs, the participants will pretend that one of them is Naomi and the other is Ruth—and they will pretend that cell phones existed in ancient Israel. They will read Ruth 2:1–23. Then they will imagine that Naomi and Ruth sent text messages to each other once every hour during the day. Using the passage, they will develop a series of text messages between Naomi and Ruth. They will present their messages by reading them aloud.

Once the pairs have had sufficient time to prepare their text messages, ask two volunteers to help hold up the cell phone they decorated during the Quick-Start Activity. Then **invite** each pair to come forward and present its text messages by putting their heads through the cell phone as they read the messages.

3. Once everybody has presented, **lead** a discussion, using these or similar questions:

   ▶ Why does Ruth go out for the day to gather grain?

   ▶ How does Boaz treat this stranger and foreigner, Ruth?

   ▶ How might we be more like Ruth?

   ▶ How might we be more like Boaz by the way we respond to those in need?

4. Then **conclude** with these or similar words:

   ▶ This story shows us how things can be when everybody acts out of love for others. Ruth shows her love by sticking with Naomi and working to gather food for them both. Naomi shows her love for Ruth by showing her where to find food and telling her how to approach Boaz. Boaz shows his love for others by going beyond what is customary and helping Ruth enormously. Look at all the good that comes out of their love: Naomi is taken care of; Boaz and Ruth eventually find love and get married; and the family line leading to King David, and ultimately to Jesus, is established. Imagine if everybody acted out of love like Ruth, Naomi, and Boaz. How amazing the world would become.

F. Announcements and Closing Prayer (5 minutes)

1. Make any needed **announcements. Assign** the background page to read and the activity to fill out for the next session if you will have the participants work on this at home.

2. **Close** with prayer by reading 1 Corinthians 13:4–6. Then say:

   ▶ God, you bless Ruth abundantly because of the faithfulness she willingly shows others. Help us to follow Ruth's example in all we do. Amen.

Chapter 10

David

Session Focus

- The participants will learn key facts about David:
    - As a young man, he defeats Goliath.
    - He is the second king of Israel and unites the twelve Tribes.
    - He is a great warrior and leader who puts his trust in God.
    - He is also a sinner who repents and asks God for forgiveness.
- The participants will study the story of David playing music for Saul and writing some of the psalms and reflect on key questions:
    - What kind of spiritual effect can music have?
    - How can any type of music enrich you spiritually?

At a Glance

A. Quick-Start Activity: Your Favorite Types of Music (5 minutes)
B. Opening Prayer Ritual (5 minutes)
C. Bible Story Sharing: The Covenant Box Is Brought to Jerusalem (10 minutes)
D. Review Student Textbook Activity Page (10 minutes)
E. Integration Activity: Music's Effect (25 minutes)
F. Announcements and Closing Prayer (5 minutes)

Preparation and Materials

Materials Needed

For each participant:
- ❏ Bible
- ❏ pencil
- ❏ handout 10–A, "Your Favorite Types of Music"

For each small group:
- ❑ paper
- ❑ pencils

Other Preparation Steps

- ❑ Mark 2 Samuel 7:8–16 in the Bible that will be used in the opening prayer ritual.
- ❑ Choose two participants to process in with the Bible and a candle for the opening prayer ritual, providing directions as needed.

Background Reading

- Read the background page for David on page 24 of the student textbook, including the suggested Bible passages.
- If you are using *Breakthrough! The Bible for Young Catholics,* read the articles "It's a Party!" located near 2 Samuel 6:12–23, and "The Power of Music," located near 1 Samuel 16:14–23.

Session Steps

A. Quick-Start Activity: Your Favorite Types of Music (5 minutes)

1. **Place** the copies of handout 10–A, "Your Favorite Types of Music," on a table along with some pencils.

2. As the participants arrive, **instruct** them each to fill out a worksheet.

B. Opening Prayer Ritual (5 minutes)

1. **Direct** the Bible bearer and candle bearer to take their places just outside the room or in the back of the room. **Gather** everyone else to stand around your prayer table. **Make** the Sign of the Cross and lead everyone in saying, "Let us remember that we are in the holy presence of God."

2. **Invite** the Bible bearer and candle bearer to silently process up to the prayer table and turn to face the group. The Bible bearer then **reads** the Scripture verse you have marked, 2 Samuel 7:8–16. When finished, the reader says, "The Word of the Lord." Everyone responds, "Thanks be to God." The Bible bearer and candle bearer then place the Bible and candle on the prayer table and go to their places.

3. Invite everyone to sit down. **Introduce** David in these or similar words:

   ▶ Today we will study King David, the greatest king of the Israelites. He has many talents. David writes music but is also a mighty warrior. Above all he has a great love for God. He is not embarrassed to express his faith in God in public, as we shall see in this passage.

C. Bible Story Sharing: The Covenant Box Is Brought to Jerusalem (10 minutes)

Note Alternative Option: Omit step C if you choose to have the participants read the background sheet in the student textbook during class. Instead, the participants would use the time to complete the reading. You may wish to use the methods outlined in Suggestions for Reading Together, in the introduction to this catechist guide.

1. **Direct** the participants to open their Bibles to 2 Samuel 6:12–22. Provide help as needed but encourage the participants to try to find the passage on their own. **Read** the passage together. See the introduction in this catechist guide for different ways to do this.

2. **Lead** the group in a short reflection on the Bible passage. If you are using *Breakthrough! The Bible for Young Catholics,* consider reading to the group the article "It's a Party!" located near this story. The following questions can help prompt discussion. Encourage all of the participants to share their thoughts.

    ▶ What is the sacred object David leads in the parade to Jerusalem? *(Answer: The Covenant Box, which is also called the Ark of the Covenant. It holds the tablets containing the Ten Commandments and represents the presence of God.)*

    ▶ How do you think you would have felt if you had seen your king or your husband dancing wildly in public wearing only his shorts?

    ▶ Are you more like Michal or more like David when it comes to practicing your faith in public? For example, are you embarrassed or proud to wear ashes on your forehead on Ash Wednesday?

3. **Summarize** the meaning of this Bible passage in these or similar words:

    ▶ David is excited about bringing the Covenant Box to his new capital city, Jerusalem. The Covenant Box will be the center of worship for all the people of Israel. With religious dancing, David leads the men carrying it. This kind of dancing is common in the Bible. But some people, like David's wife Michal, find it embarrassing. There are different ways to show our faith, and some people are more comfortable with public displays. Like David, we can refuse to let other people's opinions control our actions.

D. Review Student Textbook Activity Page (10 minutes)

Note Alternative Option: Omit step D–1 if you choose to have the participants complete the activity page at home after the session.

1. Ask the participants to **turn to the activity** on page 25 in the student textbook. Ask them to **check** their completed work as you review the answers. See the introduction in this catechist guide for suggestions on how to do this.

2. After checking the answers, **summarize** key aspects of David's life by **presenting the following points:**

    ▶ God calls David to be king when King Saul begins to disobey God. Saul tries to kill David, even though David is married to his daughter, Michal, and is best friends with Saul's son, Jonathan.

    ▶ David is a mighty warrior and leader. He unites all the tribes of Israel and makes them a unified nation.

    ▶ Even though David has a great love for God, he isn't perfect. He commits the sin of adultery with Bathsheba and later arranges for her husband to be killed. David later confesses his sin and asks God for forgiveness.

    ▶ God promises David that his descendants will rule Israel forever. This promise is fulfilled in Jesus, who is a descendant of David and who rules over all creation as our Divine King.

E. Integration Activity: Music's Effect (25 minutes)

In this activity the participants will explore their different tastes in music and the lyrics' ability to affect us spiritually. They will learn that David was a musician who wrote some of the psalms. They will then rewrite a psalm in their own words, basing it on a certain type of music.

1. **Invite** volunteers to share some of their favorite and least favorite types of music from the Quick-Start Activity. Then **lead** a discussion using these or similar questions:

    ▶ Music is a form of expression. It has a way to open up and speak what is in our hearts. What are some songs you listen to when you are happy or sad?

    ▶ How can the lyrics of those songs affect how you think or feel?

   Then **say:**

    ▶ Some lyrics can harm us spiritually. Songs that glorify violence or abuse only weaken us to the real dangers those actions involve. Some songs can help us spiritually by building us up and glorifying things that are pleasing to God. Listen to how David uses music to build someone up.

Read 1 Samuel 16:14–23. Then say:

> ▶ In addition to being a king, David is a musician. He plays the lyre, a harplike musical instrument, and some people believe David wrote some of the earliest psalms. The psalms are lyrics for hymns or songs about Israel's relationship with God. They can build us up spiritually. The psalms cover a range of topics, from praising God to crying out for help. In the Catholic Church, we sing or read the psalms as part of Mass, and they have become an important part of the way we pray. Today we are going to take a psalm and rewrite it in our own words as lyrics for a modern type of music.

2. **Place** the participants into five small groups, giving each group a sheet of paper and a pencil. **Assign** each group one of the psalms below. Tell the groups to read their psalm and then write it in their own words as lyrics for the type of music listed for their psalm.

   - Psalm 111:1–7 (Thankfulness for God's blessings—gospel)
   - Psalm 57:1–7 (A cry for help—blues)
   - Psalm 25:1–5 (Asking for guidance and direction—country)
   - Psalm 33:1–8 (A call to praise God—rap)
   - Psalm 19:1–6 (The benefits of God's laws—pop)

   After sufficient time **invite** the groups to "perform" their psalm.

3. Then **conclude** with these or similar words. If you are using *Breakthrough! The Bible for Young Catholics,* consider reading aloud the article "The Power of Music," located near 1 Samuel 16:14–23.

   > ▶ David uses music as a way to praise God and lift up others. He can teach us something about music. It does not matter what type of music you like; the lyrics can affect the music's effect on us. Some lyrics can harm us spiritually, and others can build us up. As your small groups have shown, any type of music can be used as a form of prayer. Next time you download a new song or buy a CD, ask yourself if this is a song you could listen to and sing along with that will lift you up and be a form of prayer to God.

F. Announcements and Closing Prayer (5 minutes)

1. Make any needed **announcements. Assign** the background page to read and the activity to fill out for the next session if you will have the participants work on this at home.

2. Close by **leading** the participants in a short prayer, perhaps like the following:

   > ▶ Lord, thank you for the gift of music, and help us follow David's example and let our songs always be a prayer to you. Amen.

Your Favorite Types of Music

Rate the following types of music from 1 to 20. Put the number 1 on your favorite type of music and number 20 on your least favorite type of music. Use the other numbers 2 through 19 to rank the other types. Use each number only once.

_____ rap　　　　　　　　　　_____ Christian

_____ country　　　　　　　　_____ hip hop

_____ gospel　　　　　　　　_____ rock and roll

_____ pop　　　　　　　　　_____ opera

_____ big band　　　　　　　_____ reggae

_____ 1990s　　　　　　　　_____ folk

_____ 1980s　　　　　　　　_____ heavy metal

_____ 1970s　　　　　　　　_____ classical

_____ 1960s　　　　　　　　_____ blues

_____ jazz　　　　　　　　　_____ world music

Handout 10–A: Permission to reproduce is granted. © 2010 by Saint Mary's Press.

Chapter 11

Solomon

Session Focus

- The participants will learn key facts about Solomon:
  - He is a son of David who becomes the king of Israel.
  - God grants him the gift of wisdom.
  - He is a great leader and builds the Temple to honor God.
  - He eventually turns away from God, which leads to divisions within his kingdom.
- The participants will study the Book of Proverbs and reflect on key questions:
  - How does Solomon show great wisdom?
  - How can the wisdom found in Proverbs be applied to modern life?

At a Glance

A. Quick-Start Activity: Bumper Stickers (5 minutes)
B. Opening Prayer Ritual (5 minutes)
C. Bible Story Sharing: Solomon Decides Wisely for Two Mothers (10 minutes)
D. Review Student Textbook Activity Page (10 minutes)
E. Integration Activity: Proverbs on Your Bumper (25 minutes)
F. Announcements and Closing Prayer (5 minutes)

Preparation and Materials

Materials Needed

For each participant:
- ❏ Bible and student textbook
- ❏ pencil
- ❏ sheet of 4¼-by-11-inch paper
- ❏ crayons

Other Preparation Steps

❏ Mark 1 Kings 3:10–12 in the Bible that will be used in the opening prayer ritual.

❏ Choose two participants to process in with the Bible and a candle for the opening prayer ritual, providing instructions as needed.

Background Reading

- Read the background page about Solomon on page 26 of the student textbook, including the suggested Bible passages.

Session Steps

A. Quick-Start Activity: Bumper Stickers (5 minutes)

1. **Write** the following on the board:

   - Write on the board phrases from some of your favorite bumper stickers. Don't use any that could offend others!

2. As the participants arrive, **instruct** them to follow the directions on the board.

B. Opening Prayer Ritual (5 minutes)

1. **Direct** the Bible bearer and candle bearer to take their places just outside the room or in the back of the room. **Gather** everyone else to stand around your prayer table. **Make** the Sign of the Cross and lead everyone in saying, "Let us remember that we are in the holy presence of God."

2. **Invite** the Bible bearer and candle bearer to silently process up to the prayer table and turn to face the group. The Bible bearer then **reads** the Scripture verse you have marked, 1 Kings 3:10–12. When finished, the reader says, "The Word of the Lord." Everyone responds, "Thanks be to God." The Bible bearer and candle bearer then place the Bible and candle on the prayer table and go to their places.

3. Invite everyone to sit down. **Introduce** Solomon in these or similar words:

   ▶ Today we will study King Solomon, a famous leader of God's Chosen People. He helps Israel grow as a kingdom and leads the people in building a great Temple for God. Perhaps he is best known for his wisdom. God offers Solomon anything he wants, and Solomon asks for wisdom to be a good leader. God grants Solomon his request, and Solomon uses this wisdom to decide difficult questions, as we shall see in this passage.

C. Bible Story Sharing: Solomon Decides Wisely for Two Mothers (10 minutes)

Note Alternative Option: Omit step C if you choose to have the participants read the background sheet in the student textbook during class. Instead, the participants would use the time to complete the reading. You may wish to use the methods outlined in Suggestions for Reading Together, in the introduction to this catechist guide.

1. **Direct** the participants to open their Bibles to 1 Kings 3:16–28. Provide help as needed but encourage the participants to try to find the passage on their own. **Read** the passage together. See the introduction in this catechist guide for different ways to do this.

2. **Lead** the group in a short reflection on the Bible passage. The following questions can help prompt discussion. Encourage all the participants to share their thoughts.

    ▶ What do the two women argue about before King Solomon? (Answer: Both women have recently given birth, but one of the babies has died. Both women claim to be the mother of the child still alive.)

    ▶ If you were Solomon, how might you have decided the dispute? (You may need to remind the participants that there were no DNA tests at that time.)

    ▶ Can you name situations at school, at home, or in your community where Solomon's wisdom would be helpful?

3. **Summarize** the meaning of this Bible passage in these or similar words:

    ▶ King Solomon is presented with a difficult case. Each woman claims the child is hers, and there are no other witnesses. To resolve the dispute, Solomon threatens simply to cut the child in half. At first this sounds like a disturbing solution, but it really displays Solomon's true gift of wisdom. By threatening the life of the child, Solomon reveals what is in the heart of each woman and reveals the true mother of the child. Sometimes we confront situations where it is difficult to determine who is telling the truth. We can remember that Solomon's wisdom is a gift from God, and like Solomon all we have to do is ask for it.

D. Review Student Textbook Activity Page (10 minutes)

Note Alternative Option: Omit step D–1 if you choose to have the participants complete the activity page at home after the session.

1. Ask the participants to **turn to the activity** on page 27 in the student textbook. Ask them to **check** their completed work as you review the answers. See the introduction in this catechist guide for suggestions on how to do this.

2. After checking the answers, **summarize** key aspects of Solomon's life by **presenting the following points:**

   ▶ Solomon is a son of David. Solomon becomes the third king of Israel.

   ▶ God invites Solomon to ask God for anything he wishes. Solomon asks for wisdom to be good ruler. God grants his request, and Solomon's wisdom becomes legendary.

   ▶ Solomon builds a great Temple to house the Covenant Box, or the Ark of the Covenant. The Temple provides a place to worship God.

   ▶ Solomon eventually turns away from God and begins building altars to other gods. Unfortunately, his actions lead to divisions among the People of God.

E. Integration Activity: Proverbs on Your Bumper (25 minutes)

In this activity the participants will reflect on some of their favorite bumper stickers and why bumper stickers are effective in getting messages across. The participants will then examine the Book of Proverbs and think of ways to apply its wisdom to modern life by creating bumper stickers for a proverb.

1. **Invite** volunteers to share some of the bumper stickers they wrote on the board during the Quick-Start Activity. Share some of your own favorites.

   Then **lead** a discussion using these or similar questions:

   ▶ Why do some people like bumper stickers? *(Answers may include: they provide a way to make a statement; they provide a way to be funny; they provide something to read when you are stopped at a red light.)*

   ▶ What are the qualities of a clever bumper sticker? *(Answers may include: the message often appeals to a variety of people; bumper stickers are short and to the point; they are catchy, so they are easy to remember.)*

   ▶ How do illustrations add to the bumper stickers? *(Answers may include: they help bring the phrases to life; they emphasize the point of the phrase; sometimes they add further meaning to the phrase or put a different spin on its meaning.)*

2. Then **say**:

> ▶ Some bumper stickers offer a bit of wisdom to their readers. Today we are going to make bumper stickers that offer wisdom too. We have already learned that King Solomon was a wise ruler, but did you know that the Book of Proverbs is attributed to his wisdom? Listen to the beginning of the Book of Proverbs.

Read Proverbs 1:1–6. Then **ask**:

> ▶ What does the passage say the Book of Proverbs offers readers? *(Answer: It offers understanding; it teaches how to live intelligently and justly; it can make one clever or help the wise grow wiser.)*

3. Then **say**:

> ▶ Helping people grow in wisdom sounds like a great idea, so today we are going to create bumper stickers from proverbs.

Give each participant a 4½-by-11-inch sheet of paper and some crayons. **Instruct** them to look through the Book of Proverbs and find a proverb they like that would make a good bumper sticker. Then they will design a bumper sticker for their proverb. They will help connect their proverb to modern life by the illustrations they add to their bumper stickers.

After sufficient time, **invite** volunteers to share their bumper stickers, highlighting how they have applied the stickers to modern times.

4. Then **conclude** with these or similar words:

> ▶ Although King Solomon lived long ago, your bumper stickers have shown us that the wisdom attributed to him is still relevant to us today. Perhaps this week you will take time to read a few proverbs each morning and focus on them during your day.

F. Announcements and Closing Prayer (5 minutes)

1. Make any needed **announcements**. **Assign** the background page to read and the activity to fill out for the next session if you will have the participants work on this at home.

2. Close by **leading** the participants in a short prayer, perhaps like the following:

> ▶ God, give us the gift of wisdom, as you did your servant Solomon. Amen.

Chapter 12

Isaiah

Session Focus

- The participants will learn key facts about Isaiah:
  - The Book of Isaiah was actually written by three different authors.
  - First Isaiah speaks of leadership and the perfect king.
  - Second Isaiah speaks of God's desire to comfort his people during their Exile.
  - Third Isaiah calls for justice and predicts the coming of God's perfect Kingdom.
- The participants will study stories from Isaiah and reflect on key questions:
  - What messages might the three Isaiahs bring to today's world?
  - How might you bring God's messages to others?

At a Glance

A. Quick-Start Activity: Your Own Web Page (5 minutes)
B. Opening Prayer Ritual (5 minutes)
C. Bible Story Sharing: Isaiah Predicts the Peace of Jerusalem (10 minutes)
D. Review Student Textbook Activity Page (10 minutes)
E. Integration Activity: Isaiah on the Web (25 minutes)
F. Announcements and Closing Prayer (5 minutes)

Materials and Preparation

Materials Needed

For each participant:

- ❏ Bible and student textbook
- ❏ pencil
- ❏ legal-sized sheet of paper
- ❏ colored pencils
- ❏ hymnals or songbooks with the song "Here I Am, Lord," by Dan Schutte (New Dawn Music, 1981)

For each small group:
- ❑ legal-sized piece of paper
- ❑ colored pencils

Other Preparation Steps

- ❑ Mark Isaiah 65:1 in the Bible that will be used in the opening prayer ritual.
- ❑ Choose two participants to process in with the Bible and a candle for the opening prayer ritual, providing directions as needed.

Background Reading

- Read the background page about Isaiah on page 28 of the student textbook, including the suggested Bible passages.
- If you are using *Breakthrough! The Bible for Young Catholics*, read the article "War or Peace," near Isaiah, chapter 2.

Session Steps

A. Quick-Start Activity: Your Own Web Page (5 minutes)

1. Make available sheets of legal-sized paper and colored pencils for each participant. **Write** the following on the board:

   - Use the paper and colored pencils to design your own personal Web page. Include sections like "favorites," "friends," "message board," and any others you can think of.

2. As the participants arrive, **instruct** them to follow the directions on the board.

B. Opening Prayer Ritual (5 minutes)

1. **Direct** the Bible bearer and candle bearer to take their places just outside the room or in the back of the room. **Gather** everyone else to stand around your prayer table. Make the Sign of the Cross and lead everyone in saying, "Let us remember that we are in the holy presence of God."

2. **Invite** the Bible bearer and candle bearer to silently process up to the prayer table and turn to face the group. The Bible bearer then **reads** the Scripture verse you have marked, Isaiah 65:1. When finished, the reader says, "The Word of the Lord." Everyone responds, "Thanks be to God." The Bible bearer and candle bearer then place the Bible and candle on the prayer table and go to their places.

3. **Invite** everyone to sit down. **Introduce** Isaiah in these or similar words:

▶ Today we will study the prophet Isaiah. The name Isaiah refers to three different prophets who wrote under the same name, and all shared God's Word with the Chosen People. So we will refer to all of them as Isaiah. Isaiah calls the people to follow God by living justly and hoping in God's ability to save them. Isaiah even speaks of the future when the entire world will follow God's ways, as we shall see in this passage.

C. Bible Story Sharing: Isaiah Predicts the Peace of Jerusalem (10 minutes)

Note Alternative Option: Omit step C if you choose to have the participants read the background sheet in the student textbook during class. Instead, the participants would use the time to complete the reading. You may wish to use the methods outlined in Suggestions for Reading Together, in the introduction to this catechist guide.

1. **Direct** the participants to open their Bibles to Isaiah 2:1–5. Provide help as needed but encourage the participants to try to find the passage on their own. **Read** the passage together. See the introduction in this catechist guide for different ways to do this.

2. **Lead** the group in a short reflection on the Bible passage. If you are using *Breakthrough! The Bible for Young Catholics*, consider reading aloud the article "War or Peace," located near this story. The following questions can help prompt discussion. Encourage all the participants to share their thoughts.

    ▶ What message does Isaiah give Jerusalem about the future? *(Answer: Someday, all will come to Jerusalem to learn about God and follow God's ways. Following God's ways will bring peace and put an end to all wars.)*

    ▶ Knowing that outside invaders frequently threatened Israel, how do you think the people would have responded to Isaiah's message?

    ▶ What are ways you as young people can work to bring about the peace that Isaiah speaks about?

3. **Summarize** the meaning of this Bible passage in these or similar words:

    ▶ At a time when Israel often feels threatened by other nations, Isaiah brings a message of hope from God. Isaiah speaks of a lasting peace that can happen only when everyone follows God's will. Only then will the world see an end to all wars. Isaiah's message of hope still speaks to us today. When we turn on the news, we see pictures of wars happening across the globe. It is up to us as individuals to continually work toward peace. Even if we are not presidents or kings, God still calls us to bring peace to everyone we meet. If everybody truly lives that way, then we can begin to see the peace God desires for all of us.

D. Review Student Textbook Activity Page (10 minutes)

Note Alternative Option: Omit step D–1 if you choose to have the participants complete the activity page at home after the session.

1. Ask the participants to **turn to the activity** on page 29 in the student textbook. Ask them to **check** their completed work as you review the answers. See the introduction in this catechist's guide for suggestions on how to do this.

2. After checking the answers, **summarize** key aspects of Isaiah's life by **presenting the following points:**

    ▶ Three different prophets using the same name wrote the Book of Isaiah at three different periods in Israel's history.

    ▶ First Isaiah gives advice to Israel's rulers about how to treat other nations and how to treat their subjects. He also prophesies about the coming of the ideal ruler.

    ▶ Second Isaiah lives during Israel's Exile. He speaks of a Suffering Servant who will take away Israel's suffering.

    ▶ Third Isaiah speaks of justice and a great kingdom to come after the Exile has ended.

E. Integration Activity: Isaiah on the Web (25 minutes)

In this activity the participants will share a personal Web page they will develop. Then they will explore passages from Isaiah and use them to develop a Web page for Isaiah. The participants will consider the messages Isaiah delivered and how they can deliver similar messages to the world they live in.

1. **Invite** volunteers to share their personal Web sites from the Quick-Start Activity. **Mention** that many people today use their own personal Web sites to share about themselves, their lives, and what they think is important. Today the participants will pretend they are Isaiah and develop a Web site for him.

2. **Place** the participants into small groups of three or four. Give each group a legal-sized sheet of paper and colored pencils. **Assign** each group one of the following passages:

    - Isaiah 6:1–8 (God calls Isaiah.)
    - Isaiah 44:1–5 (God consoles Israel.)
    - Isaiah 49:1–6 (Isaiah speaks of his role as a prophet.)
    - Isaiah 65:17–25 (A new Heaven and a new earth will appear.)

3. **Explain** that each small group will read its assigned passage from Isaiah. Then the groups will pretend that Isaiah has his own Web site and that they are helping him develop one of its pages to focus on the information or message in their passage. **Encourage** them to be creative. They may wish to include the same types of ideas they used for the Web page they developed earlier.

4. Once they have completed their Web page, **invite** the groups to present their work. **Ask** the groups to briefly explain their passages and how they represented them on their Web page.

5. Then **lead** a discussion using these or similar questions:

   ▶ As a prophet, what messages does Isaiah bring Israel? *(Write the participants' responses on the board.)*

   ▶ Which messages are relevant to today's society? *(Put a star by the messages they mention.)*

   ▶ Based on what you have learned about Isaiah, if he were alive today, what other messages might he bring to society? *(Add their responses to the board.)*

   Then **continue:**

   ▶ If these messages are still important, and if there are more that need to be delivered, how can we be the ones to deliver them like Isaiah?

6. **Conclude** with these or similar words:

   ▶ Isaiah places all his trust in God, which gives him the courage to speak the truth to God's people. Isaiah delivers a message of peace, justice, and hope. We too are called both to live that message and to carry it to others. We can look for ways in daily life to share the message through word and example.

F. Announcements and Closing Prayer (5 minutes)

1. Make any needed **announcements. Assign** the background page to read and the activity to fill out for the next session if you are having the participants work on this at home.

2. Close by **leading** the participants in a short prayer, giving each participant a hymnal with the song "Here I Am, Lord," by Dan Schutte. Have all the participants read or sing the song together.

Chapter 13
Ezekiel

Session Focus

- The participants will learn key facts about Ezekiel:
    - He is a prophet who uses unique ways to get people's attention.
    - He tries to warn the Israelites of the consequences of their sinfulness.
    - He brings a message of hope during a time of despair.
    - He prophesies about a New Covenant. Later Jesus fulfills this prophecy.
- The participants will study the story of God's calling of Ezekiel to be a prophet and reflect on key questions:
    - In what areas of life may God call young people to be prophets?
    - How can you have the courage and creativity to be a prophet like Ezekiel?

At a Glance

A. Quick-Start Activity: You Are What You Eat (5 minutes)
B. Opening Prayer Ritual (5 minutes)
C. Bible Story Sharing: Vision of the Dry Bones (10 minutes)
D. Review Student Textbook Activity Page (10 minutes)
E. Integration Activity: Eating a Scroll (25 minutes)
F. Announcements and Closing Prayer (5 minutes)

Materials and Preparation

Materials Needed

For each participant:
- ❏ Bible and student textbook
- ❏ paper
- ❏ pencil
- ❏ rolled fruit snack
- ❏ toothpick

Other Preparation Steps

❏ Mark Ezekiel 36:26–27 in the Bible that will be used in the opening prayer ritual.

❏ Choose two participants to process in with the Bible and a candle for the opening prayer ritual, providing directions as needed.

Background Reading

- Read the background page about Ezekiel on page 30 of the student textbook, including the suggested Bible passages.

- If you are using *Breakthrough! The Bible for Young Catholics,* read the article "Praying with New Life," located near Ezekiel, chapter 37.

Session Steps

A. Quick-Start Activity: You Are What You Eat (5 minutes)

1. **Write** the following on the board:

   ▶ You are what you eat! On a sheet of paper, list all the foods you have eaten in the last two days. Put a star by the healthy foods. Then compare your list with those of one or two others.

2. As the participants arrive, give each a sheet of paper and a pencil. **Instruct** them to follow the directions on the board.

B. Opening Prayer Ritual (5 minutes)

1. **Direct** the Bible bearer and candle bearer to take their places just outside the room or in the back of the room. **Gather** everyone else to stand around your prayer table. **Make** the Sign of the Cross and lead everyone in saying, "Let us remember that we are in the holy presence of God."

2. **Invite** the Bible bearer and candle bearer to silently process up to the prayer table and turn to face the group. The Bible bearer then **reads** the Scripture verse you have marked, Ezekiel 36:26–27. When finished, the reader says, "The Word of the Lord." Everyone responds, "Thanks be to God." The Bible bearer and candle bearer then place the Bible and candle on the prayer table and go to their places.

3. Invite everyone to sit down. **Introduce** Ezekiel in these or similar words:

   ▶ Today we will study Ezekiel, a prophet with a unique style. Ezekiel was not afraid to be different to get people's attention. He even cut off all his hair just to make a point. Ezekiel was a prophet during difficult times for Israel. The people's sinfulness had led them away from God and right into captivity. Ezekiel speaks out to them not only as a voice of warning but also as a voice of hope, as we shall see in this passage.

C. Bible Story Sharing: Vision of the Dry Bones (10 minutes)

Note Alternative Option: Omit step C if you choose to have the participants read the background sheet in the student textbook during class. Instead, the participants would use the time to complete the reading. You may wish to use the methods outlined in Suggestions for Reading Together, in the introduction to this catechist guide.

1. **Direct** the participants to open their Bibles to Ezekiel 37:1–14. Provide help as needed but encourage the participants to try to find the passage on their own. **Read** the passage together. See the introduction in this catechist guide for different ways to do this.

2. **Lead** the group in a short reflection on the Bible passage. If you are using *Breakthrough! The Bible for Young Catholics,* consider reading to the group the article "Praying with New Life," located near this story. The following questions can help prompt discussion. Encourage all the participants to share their thoughts.

   ▶ What does God tell Ezekiel to do with the dry bones? *(Answer: God tells him to prophesy to the bones and then tell the wind, God's spirit, to breathe life back into them. He does, and the bones come to life.)*

   ▶ If you were Ezekiel, would you have been afraid of the dry bones or excited to see what was happening to them?

   ▶ The dry bones symbolize a lack of hope caused by ignoring God. Where in today's world do you see a need to refocus on God and bring new hope?

3. **Summarize** the meaning of this Bible passage in these or similar words.

   ▶ What begins like a scary movie ends up being a story of hope and renewal. The Israelites have turned away from God, and as a result they have suffered greatly. Ezekiel shares his vision of the dry bones with God's people so they may find hope again. By listening to God's Word and trusting in God's Spirit, as the passage says, we too can bring hope to the world around us.

D. Review Student Textbook Activity Page (10 minutes)

Note Alternative Option: Omit step D–1 if you choose to have the participants complete the activity page at home after the session.

1. Ask the participants to **turn to the activity** on page 31 in the student textbook. Ask them to **check** their completed work as you review the answers. See the introduction in this catechist's guide for suggestions on how to do this.

2. After checking the answers, **summarize** key aspects of Ezekiel's life by **presenting the following points:**

   ▶ Ezekiel is a prophet God calls to speak out to the Israelites at a time when they have turned away from God.

   ▶ Ezekiel uses not only words but also interesting actions to get the Israelites' attention.

   ▶ Ezekiel offers a message of hope and renewal to the Israelites during the difficult time of their Exile.

   ▶ Ezekiel's prophecies of hope to Israel are fulfilled by the life, death, and Resurrection of Jesus Christ.

E. Integration Activity: Eating a Scroll (25 minutes)

In this activity the participants will consider the unusual way God gives the message Ezekiel is to speak—by directing him to eat a scroll. The participants will discuss areas in their lives where they can be prophets like Ezekiel. Then they will prayerfully focus on their own personal calling to be prophets by creating and eating their own scroll.

1. **Invite** volunteers to discuss the foods they listed during the Quick-Start Activity. Ask them to mention whether the foods are healthy. Then ask:

   ▶ How do the healthy foods make you feel?

   ▶ How do the other foods make you feel?

   Then **say:**

   ▶ The old saying "You are what you eat" is true. The foods we eat affect who we are and how we live. Ezekiel experiences this same thing but in an unusual way. Listen to how God calls Ezekiel to be a prophet.

   Summarize briefly in your own words Ezekiel 2:1–7. Then **read** Ezekiel 2:8—3:3. Afterward **ask:**

   ▶ What does Ezekiel eat, and what is written on it? *(Answer: Ezekiel eats a scroll with the words cries of grief and wails and groans. See Ezekiel 2:9.)*

   ▶ Why do you think the scroll refers to grief and wailing? *(Answer: It represents the message Ezekiel was to bring the Israelites.)*

   ▶ If you were Ezekiel, would you have eaten the scroll? Explain.

2. **Explain** that today the participants will think of ways to be a prophet like Ezekiel, and yes, they too will eat a scroll. First, **ask** them to name areas in their lives, school, or community where things are not the way God wants them to be. **Write** their responses on the board. Based on what is on the board, ask the participants to brainstorm ways they can be prophets in those situations. Remind them to be creative, because Ezekiel did not always only use words. Sometimes he was mute, and one time he cut his hair to get people's attention.

   Give each participant a rolled fruit snack and a toothpick. **Instruct** the participants to think about areas in their lives where God wants them to speak up more for the truth. Tell them to silently pray for guidance about how God wants them to be prophets in their own lives. Remind them to be creative, as Ezekiel was creative, in getting God's message across. Once they have prayed about this for a while, they will use the toothpick and etch on their rolled fruit-snack scroll a few of the main words they think God wants them to remember about how best to be prophets.

3. After sufficient time, **invite** the participants one at a time to read their scrolls aloud and eat them. Then **conclude** with these or similar words:

   ▶ Ezekiel is a brave prophet who boldly and sometimes creatively speaks up for God. It is not always easy for Ezekiel, but he remains faithful to his calling. It is not always easy for us to speak out when we see things that are not right, but we must seek the courage to be more like Ezekiel in those situations. Imagine the effect we could have if each of us fulfilled the words written on the scrolls we ate today.

F. Announcements and Closing Prayer (5 minutes)

1. Make any needed **announcements. Assign** the background page to read and the activity to fill out for the next session if you are having the participants work on this at home.

2. Close by **leading** the participants in a short prayer, perhaps like the following:

   ▶ God, you called Ezekiel to be your bold and creative prophet. Help us to courageously bring your Word to the world in new ways. Amen.

Chapter 14

Ezra and Nehemiah

Session Focus

- The participants will learn key facts about Ezra and Nehemiah:

  - They return with the Israelites to Jerusalem fifty years after it has been destroyed.

  - They lead the Israelites in physically rebuilding the Temple.

  - They lead the Israelites in spiritually rebuilding their community.

  - They help the Israelites reclaim their identity as a people based on their commitment to God.

- The participants will study the story of the Israelites' recommitment of themselves to God and reflect on key questions:

  - What religious practice or spiritual workout do the Israelites agree to follow?

  - What spiritual workout can you, as a young person, do to develop your relationship with God?

At a Glance

A. Quick-Start Activity: What a Workout! (5 minutes)

B. Opening Prayer Ritual (5 minutes)

C. Bible Story Sharing: Cyrus Sends the Jews Back to Jerusalem (10 minutes)

D. Review Student Textbook Activity Page (10 minutes)

E. Integration Activity: A Spiritual Workout: (25 minutes)

F. Announcements and Closing Prayer (5 minutes)

Materials and Preparation

Materials Needed

For each participant:

❏ Bible and student textbook

❏ pencil

For each small group:
- ❏ poster board
- ❏ markers

Other Preparation Steps

- ❏ Mark Ezra 7:10 and Nehemiah 2:17–18 in the Bible that will be used in the opening prayer ritual.
- ❏ Choose two participants to process in with the Bible and a candle for the opening prayer ritual, providing directions as needed.

Background Reading

- Read the background page about Ezra and Nehemiah on page 32 of the student text book, including the suggested Bible passages.

Session Steps

A. Quick-Start Activity: What a Workout! (5 minutes)

1. **Write** the following on the board:

    ▶ Silently complete the following: Do five pushups, then kneel and say ten Lord's Prayers. Repeat. Keep repeating until I begin class.

2. As the participants arrive, **instruct** them to follow the directions on the board.

B. Opening Prayer Ritual (5 minutes)

1. **Direct** the Bible bearer and candle bearer to take their places just outside the room or in the back of the room. **Gather** everyone else to stand around your prayer table. **Make** the Sign of the Cross and lead everyone in saying, "Let us remember that we are in the holy presence of God."

2. **Invite** the Bible bearer and candle bearer to silently process up to the prayer table and turn to face the group. The Bible bearer then **reads** the Scripture verses you have marked, Ezra 7:10 and Nehemiah 2:17–18. When finished, the reader says, "The Word of the Lord." Everyone responds, "Thanks be to God." The Bible bearer and candle bearer then place the Bible and candle on the prayer table and go to their places.

3. Invite everyone to sit down. **Introduce** Ezra and Nehemiah in these or similar words:

    ▶ Today we will study Ezra and Nehemiah, two men who have deep faith in God. These men lead the Israelites during some difficult times. The Israelites, as a people, face both physical and spiritual challenges, as we shall see in this passage.

C. Bible Story Sharing: Cyrus Sends the Jews Back to Jerusalem (10 minutes)

Note Alternative Option: Omit step C if you choose to have the participants read the background sheet in the student textbook during class. Instead, the participants would use the time to complete the reading. You may wish to use the methods outlined in Suggestions for Reading Together, in the introduction to this catechist guide.

1. **Direct** the participants to open their Bibles to Ezra 1:1–6. Provide help as needed but encourage the participants to try to find the passage on their own. **Read** the passage together. See the introduction in this catechist guide for different ways to do this.

2. **Lead** the group in a short reflection on the Bible passage. The following questions can help prompt discussion. Encourage all the participants to share their thoughts.

    ▶ What does the ruler of Persia command his people to do? *(Answer: He commands all the Israelites who have been living in exile in his kingdom to go back to Jerusalem and rebuild the Temple. He also orders the rest of his people to aid the Israelites in leaving.)*

    ▶ If your neighbors were going to return to their hometown and faced a long and difficult journey, what would you do when you heard the news? Be sad? Help them? Go with them?

    ▶ Cyrus wants the people to rebuild God's house in Jerusalem. When people's homes are devastated by hurricanes, floods, or tornadoes, what can we do to help them rebuild?

3. **Summarize** the meaning of this Bible passage in these or similar words:

    ▶ The Israelites have suffered for fifty years away from home, and during this time their home has been destroyed. The Temple, which was the center of their city and of their spiritual lives, has been ransacked and demolished to the point that they again have to lay the foundation for it. Imagine the heartbreak as they reenter Jerusalem. Words cannot describe what they see or how they feel. Many people today experience that same shock when their homes are devastated by wars or natural disasters. We are called to help people during their time of need, just as the Persian ruler ordered his people to do.

D. Review Student Textbook Activity Page (10 minutes)

Note Alternative Option: Omit step D–1 if you choose to have the participants complete the activity page at home after the session.

1. Ask the participants to **turn to the activity** on page 33 in the student textbook. Ask them to **check** their completed work as you review the answers. See the introduction in this catechist guide for suggestions on how to do this.

2. After checking the answers, **summarize** key aspects of Ezra and Nehemiah's lives by **presenting the following points:**

   ▶ After fifty years of suffering away from home, the Israelites are allowed to return to Jerusalem, but the city and Temple have been destroyed.

   ▶ Ezra and Nehemiah are men of great faith, and they lead the Israelites in their efforts to return and rebuild.

   ▶ They guide the Israelites in both physically rebuilding the Temple and spiritually recommitting themselves to God's laws.

   ▶ Together they help the Israelites reclaim their identity as a people based on their faith in God.

E. Integration Activity: A Spiritual Workout (25 minutes)

In this activity the participants will reflect on how building themselves up spiritually is similar to building themselves up physically. Then they will explore a passage from the Book of Nehemiah in which the Israelites commit themselves to living according to God's will. They will take the elements of this passage and develop a step-by-step spiritual workout plan for the Israelites. They will develop a modern spiritual workout and reflect on ways they can build themselves up spiritually.

1. Refer to the Quick-Start Activity and **ask** the following questions:

   ▶ What did you think of doing the pushups?

   ▶ What did you think of saying the Lord's Prayer?

   ▶ If you had to choose, which would you choose to do every morning?

   Then **say** these or similar words:

   ▶ Whether you want to improve yourself physically, as with pushups, or spiritually, as with praying, you need to set up a workout plan. You can work every day at your relationship with God just as you would work every day at building your muscles. After fifty years of being away from Jerusalem, the Israelites have gotten out of the habit of the spiritual workout they had when the Temple was available. Fortunately, Ezra and Nehemiah not only lead the Israelites in the physical work out of rebuilding the Temple, they also help them restore their spiritual workout.

2. **Place** the participants into small groups of three or four. Give each group a piece of poster board and markers. Instruct them to draw a vertical line down the middle of their poster

board. **Explain** that their task is to read Nehemiah 10:29–39. They will develop a step-by-step spiritual workout plan for the Israelites based on the passage. They will write their plan on the left-hand side of their poster board. Once they have completed their plan, they will use the steps they wrote on the left side to develop a modern spiritual workout plan, which they will write on the right-hand side. *(You may need to explain that the promise not to marry foreign wives in verse 30 occurs because "foreigners" may have represented people who would lead the Israelites away from God and the Covenant.)*

Once the groups have completed their posters, **invite** them to present their work. Then **lead** a discussion, using these or similar words:

> ▶ What did the Israelites agree to do to build themselves up spiritually?

> ▶ How can you build yourself up spiritually?

3. Then **invite** the participants to think of one thing they would like to focus on during the coming week to build themselves up spiritually. Ask volunteers to share their ideas. **Conclude** with these or similar words:

> ▶ The challenges the Israelites face are enormous. As a community they have been away from home for fifty years, and the home they knew has been destroyed. They are lucky to have leaders like Ezra and Nehemiah. These men help the Israelites recommit themselves to their faith in God. To do so takes work and commitment. We too can be committed and can work hard to develop our relationship with God. Like the Israelites, if we work hard, step-by-step, each day, we will see our relationship with God grow.

F. Announcements and Closing Prayer (5 minutes)

1. Make any needed **announcements. Assign** the background page to read and the activity to fill out for the next session if you will have the participants work on this at home.

2. Close by **leading** the participants in a short prayer, perhaps like the following:

> ▶ God, you sent two dedicated leaders, Ezra and Nehemiah, to help the Chosen People deepen their relationship with you. Give us the dedication and sense of commitment we need to work daily on our relationship with you. Amen.

Chapter 15

The Maccabees

Session Focus

- The participants will learn key facts about the Maccabees:
    - Mattathias and his five sons begin a revolt against a Greek king who is trying to destroy Israel's faith.
    - The revolutionaries become known as the Maccabees.
    - They inspire others to stand up for their faith, and they even die to protect it.
    - Through their leadership the Israelites are able to win their religious freedom.
- The participants will study the story of Mattathias's refusal to submit to the Greeks and reflect on key questions:
    - How does Mattathias act as a leader when confronted by temptation?
    - What riches does faithfulness offer versus the riches sinfulness offers?

At a Glance

A. Quick-Start Activity: A Mound of Temptation (5 minutes)
B. Opening Prayer Ritual (5 minutes)
C. Bible Story Sharing: Antiochus Persecutes the Jews (10 minutes)
D. Review Student Textbook Activity Page (10 minutes)
E. Integration Activity: Tear Down the Mound of Temptation (25 minutes)
F. Announcements and Closing Prayer (5 minutes)

Materials and Preparation

Materials Needed

For each participant:
- ❏ Bible and student textbook
- ❏ pencil
- ❏ gray and brown crayons
- ❏ scissors

Additional materials:
- ☐ tape

Other Preparation Steps

- ☐ Mark 2 Maccabees 10:1–3 in the Bible that will be used in the opening prayer ritual.
- ☐ Choose two participants to process in with the Bible and a candle for the opening prayer ritual, providing directions as needed.
- ☐ On a sheet of paper, draw the outline of an oval-shaped stone. Make enough copies of it so each participant receives two "stones."

Background Reading

- Read the background page about the Maccabees on page 34 of the student textbook, including the suggested Bible passages.

Session Steps

A. Quick-Start Activity: A Mound of Temptation (5 minutes)

1. Have available gray and brown crayons, scissors, and the copies of the outlines of the stones you have prepared. **Write** the following on the board:

    ▶ Take two sheets with the stone outline on them. Cut out the stones. On each stone write down one thing that is a temptation to young people. Finally, color your stones, using the crayons to make them look real.

2. As the participants arrive, **instruct** them to follow the directions on the board. Once participants have completed writing on their stones, have them **tape** the stones to the wall in the shape of a mound.

B. Opening Prayer Ritual (5 minutes)

1. **Direct** the Bible bearer and candle bearer to take their places just outside the room or in the back of the room. **Gather** everyone else to stand around your prayer table. **Make** the Sign of the Cross and lead everyone in saying, "Let us remember that we are in the holy presence of God."

2. **Invite** the Bible bearer and candle bearer to silently process up to the prayer table and turn to face the group. The Bible bearer then **reads** the Scripture verse you have marked, 2 Maccabees 10:1–3. When finished, the reader says, "The Word of the Lord." Everyone responds, "Thanks be to God." The Bible bearer and candle bearer then place the Bible and candle on the prayer table and go to their places.

3. Invite everyone to sit down. **Introduce** the Maccabees in these or similar words:

   ▶ Today we will study the Maccabees. They were a group of Israelite rebels led by a man named Mattathias and his five sons. They are known for fighting to protect their faith in God. The need for their courage and determination arises out of an unbelievable situation, as we shall see in this passage.

C. Bible Story Sharing: Antiochus Persecutes the Jews (10 minutes)

Note Alternative Option: Omit step C if you choose to have the participants read the background sheet in the student textbook during class. Instead, the participants would use the time to complete the reading. You may wish to use the methods outlined in Suggestions for Reading Together, in the introduction to this catechist guide.

1. **Direct** the participants to open their Bibles to 1 Maccabees 1:20–25,41–50. Provide help as needed but encourage the participants to try to find the passage on their own. **Read** the passage together. See the introduction in this catechist guide for different ways to do this.

2. **Lead** the group in a short reflection on the Bible passage. The following questions can help prompt discussion. Encourage all the participants to share their thoughts.

   ▶ What does King Antiochus do to the Temple and the religious practices of the Israelites? *(Answer: He steals all the valuables from the Temple. He also orders the Israelites to stop practicing their faith and orders them to worship pagan gods.)*

   ▶ If you were an Israelite living in Jerusalem at the time, and you saw the destruction of the Temple and the end of your religious practices, what would you have done?

   ▶ If this happened to our Church, what would upset you more—the destruction of the church building or the decree ending all religious practices? Why?

3. **Summarize** the meaning of this Bible passage in these or similar words:

   ▶ The actions of King Antiochus are so terrible, it is hard to imagine how devastated the Israelites must be by the loss of their Temple and the decree to give up their religious practices. They are left with the choice to leave their religion behind or to keep it at great personal risk. Such a choice forces people to consider what is truly important to them about their faith. We can all ask ourselves similar questions: What is important enough about following Jesus for us to risk everything? At what point do we speak out against things that go against our faith even if it means personal risk?

D. Review Student Textbook Activity Page (10 minutes)

Note Alternative Option: Omit step D–1 if you choose to have the participants complete the activity page at home after the session.

1. Ask the participants to **turn to the activity** on page 35 in the student textbook. Ask them to **check** their completed work as you review the answers. See the introduction in this catechist's guide for suggestions on how to do this.

2. After checking the answers, **summarize** key aspects of the Maccabees by **presenting the following points:**

    ▶ The Maccabees are a group of rebels who stand up against a Greek king, because he has destroyed the Temple and ordered the Israelites to worship pagan gods.

    ▶ Mattathias and his five sons lead the Maccabees. They lead the Israelites in battle, often attacking with great power.

    ▶ Many others are inspired to take up the fight and are willing to die rather than turn from God and the practice of their religion.

    ▶ Despite the risk, the Maccabees fight fiercely to protect their religion and inspire all Israel to keep the faith.

E. Integration Activity: Tear Down the Mound of Temptation (25 minutes)

In this activity the participants will reflect on temptations young people experience. Then they will explore Mattathias's decision as a leader to resist temptation and refuse to abandon his faith. They will tear down their mound of temptation and rebuild it, as the Maccabees did, from stones marked with leadership and the true rewards of faith.

1. **Invite** volunteers to share temptations they listed on their stones during the Quick-Start Activity. Mention how the shape of their mound of temptations is similar to the shape of an outside altar mentioned in the Book of Maccabees. Invite them to open their Bibles to 1 Maccabees 2:15–28. Ask a volunteer to **read** the passage aloud.

    Then **lead** a discussion, using these or similar questions:

    ▶ Why does the official want Mattathias to offer a sacrifice on the altar? *(Answer: Because Mattathias is a leader, and others will offer sacrifice if he does.)* Think about ways you are a leader and how you may influence others.

    ▶ What does the official offer Mattathias if he offers the sacrifice? *(Answer: He offers Mattathias gold and riches as well as offering him and his sons the title "Friends of the King.")* Look at the stones on our wall. What "gold and many gifts" do they offer people?

▶ What does Mattathias do instead of accepting the official's offer? *(Answer: He kills the official and destroys the altar.)*

2. Then **say** these or similar words:

▶ If Mattathias destroys the altar because it represents temptation and sin, then we too can take down our mound. I invite each of you to carefully take any two of the stones from the wall and then return to your seat.

Then **tell** the participants that on the back of one of their stones they will write ways they can be leaders like Mattathias. On the back of the other stone, they will write rewards that faithfulness will give them. Once they have finished writing, ask them to use the crayons to color their stones to look like real stones.

Once the participants have finished, **explain** that after much struggle, the Maccabees recapture the Temple and hold a special ceremony to rededicate it to God. **Read** 2 Maccabees 10:1–8. Then **say** these or similar words:

▶ We too can rebuild our mound so it represents not sin and temptation but rather the best of our faith.

Invite the participants to come forward to read what they have written on their two stones and then tape them to the wall again, this time with the leadership ideas and rewards of faith visible.

3. Then **conclude** with these or similar words:

▶ The official singles out Mattathias because he is a leader. As a leader, Mattathias understands the importance of his decision. If he chooses to give in and renounce his faith, his sons will do the same, and there will be no revolt. By refusing, Mattathias encourages countless others to fight for their faith. There are times when we are leaders and must choose between right and wrong. In those cases we can pray for the courage and conviction of Mattathias, knowing that the true rewards are those that come from living out our faith.

F. Announcements and Closing Prayer (5 minutes)

1. Make any needed **announcements. Assign** the background page to read and the activity to fill out for the next session if you will have the participants work on this at home.

2. Close by **leading** the participants in a short prayer, perhaps like the following:

▶ God, you inspired Mattathias and the Maccabees to show great courage and conviction. Give us the strength we need to stand up for what is right and live according to your will. Amen.

Chapter 16

Introduction to the New Testament

Session Focus

- The participants will learn key facts about the New Testament:

  - It is made up of twenty-seven books that center on Jesus.

  - It contains several kinds of writing, like the Gospels and letters.

  - It shows how Jesus fulfills the promises made in the Old Testament and offers salvation to the entire world.

  - It can be divided into three main sections.

- The participants will learn about the structure of the New Testament and reflect on key questions:

  - How do all the books of the New Testament proclaim Jesus by teaching us about him and encouraging us to follow him?

  - How can you proclaim Jesus to others?

At a Glance

A. Quick-Start Activity: New Testament Things in Common (5 minutes)

B. Opening Prayer Ritual (5 minutes)

C. Bible Story Sharing: The Conclusion of the Gospel of John (10 minutes)

D. Review Student Textbook Activity Page (10 minutes)

E. Integration Activity: Proclaiming Jesus (25 minutes)

F. Announcements and Closing Prayer (5 minutes)

Materials and Preparation

Materials Needed

For each participant:

❏ Bible and student textbook

❏ pencil

❏ handout 16–A, "New Testament Things in Common"

For each small group:
- ❏ sheet of easel-sized paper
- ❏ markers
- ❏ scissors

Other Preparation Steps

- ❏ Mark Luke 1:1–4 in the Bible that will be used in the opening prayer ritual.
- ❏ Choose two participants to process in with the Bible and a candle for the opening prayer ritual, providing directions as needed.
- ❏ Copy the lists on handout 16–A, "New Testament Things in Common," so there are enough half sheets for each participant. Cut them as directed on the handout.

Background Reading

- Read the background page about the New Testament on page 36 of the student textbook.

Session Steps

A. Quick-Start Activity: New Testament Things in Common (5 minutes)

1. Have available pencils and copies of handout 16–A, "New Testament Things in Common." **Write** the following on the board:

    ▶ Individually or in small groups complete the handout "New Testament Things in Common."

2. As the participants arrive, **instruct** them to follow the directions on the board.

B. Opening Prayer Ritual (5 minutes)

1. **Direct** the Bible bearer and candle bearer to take their places just outside the room or in the back of the room. **Gather** everyone else to stand around your prayer table. **Make** the Sign of the Cross and lead everyone in saying, "Let us remember that we are in the holy presence of God."

2. **Invite** the Bible bearer and candle bearer to silently process up to the prayer table and turn to face the group. The Bible bearer then **reads** the Scripture verse you have marked, Luke 1:1–4. When finished, the reader says, "The Word of the Lord." Everyone responds, "Thanks be to God." The Bible bearer and candle bearer then place the Bible and candle on the prayer table and go to their places.

3. Invite everyone to sit down. **Introduce** the New Testament in these or similar words:

   ▶ Today we will learn about the New Testament. It is the collection of books, inspired by God, that teach us about Jesus and encourage us to follow him. They tell us of his life, death, and Resurrection. They also guide us in how to be a follower of Jesus and what to expect when he returns. When your topic is the Son of God, one could always say more about him, as we shall see in this passage.

C. Bible Story Sharing: The Conclusion of the Gospel of John (10 minutes)

Note Alternative Option: Omit step C if you choose to have the participants read the background sheet in the student textbook during class. Instead, the participants would use the time to complete the reading. You may wish to use the methods outlined in Suggestions for Reading Together, in the introduction to this catechist guide.

1. **Direct** the participants to open their Bibles to John 21:25. Provide help as needed but encourage the participants to try to find the passage on their own. **Read** the passage together. See the introduction in this catechist guide for different ways to do this.

2. **Lead** the group in a short reflection on the Bible passage. The following questions can help prompt discussion. Encourage all the participants to share their thoughts.

   ▶ At the end of his Gospel, what does John say about Jesus and the Gospel? *(Answer: John says that all the books in the world could not contain an account of everything Jesus did.)*

   ▶ If you were John and writing a Gospel, what type of information about Jesus might you want to include? *(Possible answers: physical appearance, childhood stories, Crucifixion accounts.)*

   ▶ What are some ways you can learn more about Jesus?

3. **Summarize** the meaning of this Bible passage in these or similar words:

   ▶ In completing the Gospel, John ends by saying that much more could be said of Jesus and the things he did. It leaves us readers wondering what else John might have been thinking about. Perhaps that is one of those questions we will have answered once we enter Heaven. For now we have the Gospels and the rest of the New Testament to give us more than enough to read and think about. Just consider that these twenty-seven books have inspired people for more than two thousand years to have faith in Jesus.

D. Review Student Textbook Activity Page (10 minutes)

Note Alternative Option: Omit step D–1 if you choose to have the participants complete the activity page at home after the session.

1. Ask the participants to **turn to the activity** on page 37 in the student textbook. Ask them to **check** their completed work as you review the answers. See the introduction in this catechist's guide for suggestions on how to do this.

2. After checking the answers, **summarize** key aspects of the New Testament by **presenting the following points:**

    ▶ The New Testament contains twenty-seven books, all of which were inspired by the Holy Spirit and focus on the life, death, and Resurrection of Jesus Christ.

    ▶ The New Testament shows how Jesus fulfilled the promises made to the Israelites and opened God's offer of salvation to the world.

    ▶ The New Testament shows how, through faith in Jesus Christ, we can be freed from sin and death and find eternal life.

    ▶ The New Testament can be divided into three main sections: the Gospels and Acts; the letters; and the Book of Revelation. Each section contains different types of information about Jesus.

E. Integration Activity: Proclaiming Jesus (25 minutes)

In this activity the participants will consider how the books of the New Testament proclaim Jesus in some way. In groups the participants will explore the New Testament and decorate a microphone based on things they find that teach us about Jesus or encourage us to follow him. Then they will consider ways they can proclaim Jesus to others.

1. **Ask** the participants to look at the list found on handout 16–A, "New Testament Things in Common," from the Quick-Start Activity. **Ask** volunteers to share their answers with the other participants. The correct answers are listed below:

    1. Gold, Frankincense, Myrrh: <u>Gifts of the Magi</u>

    2. Field, Tomb, Wilderness: <u>Places angels appeared</u>

    3. Sandals, Cloak, Robe: <u>Clothing of Jesus specifically mentioned in the Bible</u>

    4. Elijah, Jeremiah, Gardener: <u>Mistaken identities of Jesus</u>

    5. Rome, Thessalonica, Ephesus: <u>Names of cities with churches addressed in New Testament letters</u>

    6. Sheep, Fish, Birds: <u>Animals mentioned in Jesus' parables</u>

    7. Tax collector, Fisherman, Twin: <u>People Jesus called to be Apostles</u>

    8. Boat, Mount, Temple: <u>Places from which Jesus taught</u>

9. Dragon, White Horse, Lamb: <u>Symbolic animals mentioned in the Book of Revelation</u>

10. Gospels, Letters, Revelation: <u>Teach us about Jesus and encourage us to follow him</u>

Then **say** these or similar words:

> ▶ The sets of three we discussed are taken from the New Testament, but now we are going to focus our attention on the last three. The Gospels, the letters, and the Book of Revelation all, in their own ways, teach us about Jesus and encourage us to follow him. Today we will examine the different sections of the New Testament and see what they proclaim about Jesus.

Place the participants in three groups. Give each group a sheet of easel-sized paper, markers, and scissors. Instruct each group to draw a giant microphone (with the middle open so they can write in it). Have them cut out their microphones. Then assign each group one of the following three topics: Gospels, letters, and the Book of Revelation. Tell them to write the name of their topic in the middle of their microphone.

Instruct each group to flip through its section of the Bible and look for stories or phrases that proclaim something about Jesus. The passage can be words that encourage us to follow Jesus or teach us something about him. Once the groups have found some words, they will write phrases or draw pictures on their microphones of what they have found.

After sufficient time, **invite** the groups to present their microphones. Then **say** these or similar words:

> ▶ As the stories and information in the New Testament proclaim Jesus, so we are called to proclaim Jesus by teaching what we know about him and encouraging others to follow him. What are some ways you, as young people, can proclaim Jesus?

Then **conclude** with these or similar words:

> ▶ It is amazing when you stop to think about all the different things the New Testament proclaims about Jesus. Knowing that Jesus desires a full relationship with us, it only makes sense that the New Testament teaches and encourages us in so many different ways. As followers of Jesus, our responsibility is to read the New Testament so we can learn more about Jesus, learn to be one of his followers, and proclaim Jesus to others. I encourage each of you to set a goal for yourself to take some time at home to read more about Jesus.

F. Announcements and Closing Prayer (5 minutes)

1. Make any needed **announcements. Assign** the background page to read and the activity to fill out for the next session if you will have the participants work on this at home.

2. Close by **leading** the participants in a short prayer, perhaps like the following:

> ▶ God, thank you so much for the gift of the New Testament. Help us use it wisely as we seek to learn more about your son, Jesus. Amen.

New Testament Things in Common

Read each set of three people, places, or things found in the New Testament and determine what the three have in common. Write your answers on the blanks provided.

1. Gold, Frankincense, Myrrh
   _____

2. Field, Tomb, Wilderness
   _____

3. Sandals, Cloak, Robe
   _____

4. Elijah, Jeremiah, Gardener
   _____

5. Rome, Thessalonica, Ephesus
   _____

6. Sheep, Fish, Birds
   _____

7. Tax collector, Fisherman, Twin
   _____

8. Boat, Mount, Temple
   _____

9. Dragon, White Horse, Lamb
   _____

10. Gospels, Letters, Revelation
    _____

Read each set of three people, places, or things found in the New Testament and determine what the three have in common. Write your answers on the blanks provided.

1. Gold, Frankincense, Myrrh
   _____

2. Field, Tomb, Wilderness
   _____

3. Sandals, Cloak, Robe
   _____

4. Elijah, Jeremiah, Gardener
   _____

5. Rome, Thessalonica, Ephesus
   _____

6. Sheep, Fish, Birds
   _____

7. Tax collector, Fisherman, Twin
   _____

8. Boat, Mount, Temple
   _____

9. Dragon, White Horse, Lamb
   _____

10. Gospels, Letters, Revelation
    _____

Handout 16–A: Permission to reproduce is granted. © 2010 by Saint Mary's Press.

Chapter 17

Mary of Nazareth

Session Focus

- The participants will learn key facts about Mary of Nazareth:
  - She is a young teenage girl who boldly accepts God's will for her.
  - While engaged to Joseph and remaining a virgin, she conceives God's Son, Jesus.
  - She encourages Jesus to perform his first miracle at Cana and instructs the servants to simply do whatever he tells them.
  - She supports her son throughout his ministry.
- The participants will study the story of the Annunciation and reflect on key questions:
  - As a young person much like you, what emotions might Mary have experienced on hearing such overwhelming news?
  - How can you look to Mary's example of trusting in God when God challenges you to do something difficult?

At a Glance

A. Quick-Start Activity: The Art Gallery (5 minutes)
B. Opening Prayer Ritual (5 minutes)
C. Bible Story Sharing: The Wedding at Cana (10 minutes)
D. Review Student Textbook Activity Page (10 minutes)
E. Integration Activity: A Poem about Mary (25 minutes)
F. Announcements and Closing Prayer (5 minutes)

Materials and Preparation

Materials Needed

For each participant:
- ❏ Bible and student textbook
- ❏ pencil
- ❏ paper
- ❏ copy of the Hail Mary for closing prayer

Additional materials:

- ❏ slips of paper, each with a different letter of the alphabet on it, one for each participant (Do not include the letters x or z. If you have more than twenty-four participants, duplicate letters.)
- ❏ four different images of the Annunciation. An Internet search can yield several possibilities.
- ❏ four sheets of easel-sized paper

Other Preparation Steps

- ❏ Mark Luke 1:46–55 in the Bible that will be used in the opening prayer ritual.
- ❏ Choose two participants to process in with the Bible and a candle for the opening prayer ritual, providing directions as needed.
- ❏ Mount four different images of the Annunciation, one each in the center of the four different sheets of easel-sized paper. Hang them in four different locations in your classroom.

Background Reading

- Read the background page about Mary of Nazareth on page 38 of the student textbook, including the suggested Bible passages.
- If you are using *Breakthrough! The Bible for Young Catholics*, read the article "Mary as the First Disciple," located near John 2:1–12.

Session Steps

A. Quick-Start Activity: The Art Gallery (5 minutes)

1. **Write** the following on the board:

    ▶ Look at the four pictures of the angel telling Mary she will become the Mother of God. On the border of the one you like best, write three emotions that come to mind when you look at the people in the picture.

2. As the participants arrive, **instruct** them to follow the directions on the board.

B. Opening Prayer Ritual (5 minutes)

1. **Direct** the Bible bearer and candle bearer to take their places just outside the room or in the back of the room. **Gather** everyone else to stand around your prayer table. **Make** the Sign of the Cross and lead everyone in saying, "Let us remember that we are in the holy presence of God."

2. **Invite** the Bible bearer and candle bearer to silently process up to the prayer table and turn to face the group. The Bible bearer then **reads** the Scripture verse you have marked, Luke 1:46–55. When finished, the reader says, "The Word of the Lord." Everyone responds, "Thanks be to God." The Bible bearer and candle bearer then place the Bible and candle on the prayer table and go to their places.

3. Invite everyone to sit down. **Introduce** Mary of Nazareth in these or similar words:

   ▶ Today we will study Mary of Nazareth. Mary is a young teenage girl who loves God and bravely follows his will for her. This young girl courageously accepts her role as the Mother of Jesus, the Son of God. During her life on earth, she cares for Jesus and actively leads others to him, as we shall see in this passage.

C. Bible Story Sharing: The Wedding at Cana (10 minutes)

Note Alternative Option: Omit step C if you choose to have the participants read the background sheet in the student textbook during class. Instead, the participants would use the time to complete the reading. You may wish to use the methods outlined in Suggestions for Reading Together, in the introduction to this catechist guide.

1. **Direct** the participants to open their Bibles to John 2:1–12. Provide help as needed but encourage the participants to try to find the passage on their own. **Read** the passage together. See the introduction in this catechist guide for different ways to do this.

2. **Lead** the group in a short reflection on the Bible passage. If you are using *Breakthrough! The Bible for Young Catholics,* consider reading to the group the article "Mary as the First Disciple," located near this story. The following questions can help prompt discussion. Encourage all the participants to share their thoughts.

   ▶ Why does Mary tell the servants to listen to Jesus? *(Answer: They are out of wine for the wedding reception, and she knows Jesus can perform a miracle.)*

   ▶ If you were one of the servants, what would you have thought about Mary and Jesus when you realized what had happened to the water you just poured into the jars?

   ▶ Who in your life is like Mary, pointing you toward Jesus and saying, "Do whatever he tells you" (John 2:5)? What characteristics does that person have?

3. **Summarize** the meaning of this Bible passage in these or similar words:

   ▶ Running out of wine during the wedding reception would be very embarrassing for the wedding couple and the couple's families. Seeing the problem, Mary boldly steps forward and encourages her son, Jesus, to perform his first miracle. As a result, the couple is spared the embarrassment, and Jesus begins his public ministry. Through Mary's directions to the servants, we learn about her role in leading others to Jesus. Mary simply points them to Jesus and says, "Do whatever he tells you." We too can be like the servants—we can follow Jesus and do whatever he tell us to do.

D. Review Student Textbook Activity Page (10 minutes)

Note Alternative Option: Omit step D–1 if you choose to have the participants complete the activity page at home after the session.

1. Ask the participants to **turn to the activity** on page 39 in the student textbook. Ask them to **check** their completed work as you review the answers. See the introduction in this catechist's guide for suggestions on how to do this.

2. After checking the answers, **summarize** key aspects of Mary of Nazareth's life by **presenting the following points:**

    ▶ Mary is a young teenage girl engaged to a carpenter named Joseph, who is a descendant of King David.

    ▶ An angel tells Mary she will maintain her virginity and by the power of the Holy Spirit will conceive and give birth to the Son of God.

    ▶ Mary shows remarkable courage by saying yes to God's plan for her.

    ▶ Mary is present throughout Jesus' life, not only at his birth, but for his first miracle, for his death on the cross, and for his sending of the Holy Spirit down on the Apostles at Pentecost.

E. Integration Activity: A Poem about Mary (25 minutes)

In this activity the participants will consider the range of emotions Mary might have experienced during the Annunciation. In the face of those emotions, Mary shows great courage and faith in God. At times we may feel God is asking the impossible of us, but we can look to Mary's example of courage and trust for encouragement.

1. **Walk** to each of the four pictures of the Annunciation from the Quick-Start Activity. Randomly call out an emotion written on the art by one of the participants. **Ask** who wrote it and why the person chose that emotion.

2. Then **say** these or similar words:

    ▶ These pictures show not only a big decision for Mary, but a history-making decision. Imagine the joy and fear in saying yes to becoming the Mother of God! Keep in mind that when Mary is greeted by the angel, she is only a young person much like you. She still lives at home with her parents and is engaged, or betrothed, to Joseph. Because she is not yet married, it would be assumed that she is still a virgin, so being pregnant would not only be shameful, but under Jewish law it could lead to her being stoned to death.

3. Ask a volunteer to read Luke 1:26–38. Then ask the following questions:

    ▶ Mary asks the angel questions. What questions would you have asked the angel?

    ▶ If you were Mary, would you have said yes? Explain.

    ▶ After the angel leaves, Mary is alone. What do you believe she thinks and feels? Who do you think she will turn to for advice and support? Who would you turn to if you were in that situation?

4. **Give** each participant a sheet of paper, a pencil, and a slip of paper with one letter of the alphabet on it. On the larger sheet of paper, **instruct** the participants to write a seven-line poem about the Annunciation based on their discussion. They will begin each line of their poem with the letter of the alphabet they have been given.

5. After sufficient time, **invite** volunteers to share their poems. Then **conclude** with these or similar words:

    ▶ During times in your life when you feel God asks the impossible of you or fear prevents you from following Jesus, remember Mary. When God called her, she was a young person like you. She took a risk by simply trusting God, and she became the greatest woman in all history.

F. Announcements and Closing Prayer (5 minutes)

1. Make any needed **announcements. Assign** the background page to read and the activity to fill out for the next session if you will have the participants work on this at home.

2. Close by handing out copies of the Hail Mary and **leading** the participants in praying it together.

Chapter 18

John the Baptist

Session Focus

- The participants will learn key facts about John the Baptist:
    - Before John is born, God has a great plan for his life.
    - He boldly proclaims a message of repentance.
    - He heralds the coming of the Messiah.
    - He dies for speaking the truth to a king.
- The participants will study the story of John's preaching in the desert and reflect on key questions:
    - How can his message be applied to modern audiences?
    - How might you work to proclaim John's message of repentance?

At a Glance

A. Quick-Start Activity: Slogans (5 minutes)
B. Opening Prayer Ritual (5 minutes)
C. Bible Story Sharing: The Announcement of John's Birth (10 minutes)
D. Review Student Textbook Activity Page (10 minutes)
E. Integration Activity: John's Modern Billboard (25 minutes)
F. Announcements and Closing Prayer (5 minutes)

Materials and Preparation

Materials Needed

For each participant:
- ❏ Bible and student textbook
- ❏ pencil
- ❏ copy of an "Act of Contrition" for closing prayer

For each small group:
- ❑ sheet of easel-sized paper
- ❑ markers

Other Preparation Steps

- ❑ Mark Isaiah 40:3 in the Bible that will be used in the opening prayer ritual.
- ❑ Choose two participants to process in with the Bible and a candle for the opening prayer ritual, providing directions as needed.

Background Reading

- Read the background page about John the Baptist on page 40 of the student textbook, including the suggested Bible passages.

Session Steps

A. Quick-Start Activity: Slogans (5 minutes)

1. **Write** the following on the board:

    ▶ On the board write some of your favorite slogans or sayings from commercials.

2. As the participants arrive, **instruct** them to follow the directions on the board.

B. Opening Prayer Ritual (5 minutes)

1. **Direct** the Bible bearer and candle bearer to take their places just outside the room or in the back of the room. **Gather** everyone else to stand around your prayer table. **Make** the Sign of the Cross and lead everyone in saying, "Let us remember that we are in the holy presence of God."

2. **Invite** the Bible bearer and candle bearer to silently process up to the prayer table and turn to face the group. The Bible bearer then **reads** the Scripture verse you have marked, Isaiah 40:3. When finished, the reader says, "The Word of the Lord." Everyone responds, "Thanks be to God." The Bible bearer and candle bearer then place the Bible and candle on the prayer table and go to their places.

3. Invite everyone to sit down. **Introduce** John the Baptist in these or similar words:

    ▶ Today we will study John the Baptist, the man God calls to help prepare his people for the coming of the Messiah. John wears unique clothing and lives a unique life. He is bold when delivering God's message. His life fulfills a promise an angel made to his father, as we shall see in this passage.

C. Bible Story Sharing: The Announcement of John's Birth (10 minutes)

Note Alternative Option: Omit step C if you choose to have the participants read the background sheet in the student textbook during class. Instead, the participants would use the time to complete the reading. You may wish to use the methods outlined in Suggestions for Reading Together, in the introduction to this catechist guide.

1. **Direct** the participants to open their Bibles to Luke 1:8–17. Provide help as needed but encourage the participants to try to find the passage on their own. **Read** the passage together. See the introduction in this catechist guide for different ways to do this.

2. **Lead** the group in a short reflection on the Bible passage. The following questions can help prompt discussion. Encourage all the participants to share their thoughts.

    ▶ What does the angel tell Zechariah about his son, John? *(Answer: John will bring much joy; he will lead many people to follow God once again; he will prepare the people for the coming of the Lord.)*

    ▶ Zechariah and his wife, Elizabeth, are too old to have children. If you were Zechariah, how would you have felt hearing all this about your future son?

    ▶ You know God has a plan for every person. If you were going to have a child, what do you think an angel might tell you about your future son or daughter? How would you help fulfill God's plan for your child?

3. **Summarize** the meaning of this Bible passage in these or similar words:

    ▶ Zechariah and Elizabeth are faithful people. Although old, they have prayed to have a son. God graciously answers their prayers. As the angel explains, God has great plans for their son, John. He will help bring the people of Israel closer to God. Most important, John will herald the coming of the Messiah, Jesus. God has a plan for each of us, just like John. It is up to us to seek and follow God's will for us and to help others follow God's will for them. By doing so, who knows—we too may be called to do extraordinary things like John.

D. Review Student Textbook Activity Page (10 minutes)

Note Alternative Option: Omit step D–1 if you choose to have the participants complete the activity page at home after the session.

1. Ask the participants to **turn to the activity** on page 41 in the student textbook. Ask them to **check** their completed work as you review the answers. See the introduction in this catechist guide for suggestions on how to do this.

2. After checking the answers, **summarize** key aspects of John the Baptist's life by **presenting the following points:**

   ▶ John is Jesus' cousin. From the time of John's birth, God declared that John's role is to prepare people for the coming of Jesus, the Messiah.

   ▶ John lives in the desert, where he lives a simple life eating locusts and wild honey. Many people come to hear him preach about the coming of the Kingdom of God and the need to repent.

   ▶ John baptizes people in the Jordan River as a sign of their repentance. When Jesus comes to be baptized, John does not want to do it, because Jesus is sinless and greater than John, but John does it anyway. When he does, the Holy Spirit descends on Jesus and a voice from Heaven identifies him as God's own beloved Son.

   ▶ King Herod kills John for speaking the truth about Herod's sinful relationship with his brother's wife.

E. Integration Activity: John's Modern Billboard (25 minutes)

In this activity the participants will consider the message that John the Baptist cries out in the desert. They will consider ways John's message can be addressed to today's audiences. They will then reflect on the need for John's message today and their role in proclaiming it.

1. **Invite** volunteers to share some of their favorite sayings from the Quick-Start Activity. Ask them to explain why they like a particular saying. Then **explain** with these or similar words:

   ▶ Often, good slogans are catchy or touch people in a striking way. John the Baptist had his own slogan. Today we will study his slogan and modernize it for today's audiences.

   Have the participants open their Bibles to Matthew 3:1–2 and follow along as you read it. **Ask** the following question:

   ▶ The slogan John used in his preaching was "Turn away from your sins, because the Kingdom of Heaven is near!" What does that phrase mean?

   Have the participants turn to Luke 3:10–14 and **say:**

   ▶ While John preached his message, many different people came out to see him. Listen to how John adapted his message for different groups of people.

   Read Luke 3:10–14.

2. **Place** the participants into small groups of three or four. Give each group a sheet of easel-sized paper and markers. **Assign** each group one of the following topics or develop your own list: rap stars, celebrities, team captains, teachers, parents, or young people. **Instruct** the groups to come up with a modern message John might have for their assigned group of people. Once the group members agree on a message, they will use the easel-sized paper and design a highway billboard to display their message. Encourage them to be creative with their billboard. Often it's the artwork that draws attention to the message.

After sufficient time, **invite** the groups to share their billboards with the class. Then **lead** a discussion, using these or similar questions:

▶ Has the need for John's message changed much over the years?

▶ Would you be willing to stand up in a crowd and proclaim your message to them? How do you think people would react to you?

▶ How can you proclaim John's message to today's world?

Then **conclude** with these or similar words:

▶ John the Baptist is a bold man who bravely speaks the truth. He challenges the people of his time to turn away from sin and follow God. We are called to be like John. We can pray for the courage to boldly speak the truth even if it is not popular.

F. Announcements and Closing Prayer (5 minutes)

1. Make any needed **announcements. Assign** the background page to read and the activity to fill out for the next session if you will have the participants work on this at home.

2. Close by handing out copies of an "Act of Contrition" and **leading** everyone in praying it together.

Chapter 19

Jesus and His Family

Session Focus

- The participants will learn key facts about Jesus Christ and his family:
  - Mary and Joseph willingly agree to be a part of God's plan for the birth of the Savior, Jesus.
  - King Herod seeks to kill the infant Jesus, causing the family to flee.
  - As a young person, Jesus is aware of his mission to do God's work.
  - Jesus is both true God and true human.
- The participants will study the stories from Jesus' childhood and reflect on key questions:
  - What is Jesus' experience of family as a young child?
  - How is Jesus' experience of family like your own experience?

At a Glance

A. Quick-Start Activity: Family Photo Album (5 minutes)
B. Opening Prayer Ritual (5 minutes)
C. Bible Story Sharing: The Escape to Egypt (10 minutes)
D. Review Student Workbook Activity Page (10 minutes)
E. Integration Activity: Jesus' Family Photo Album (25 minutes)
F. Announcements and Closing Prayer (5 minutes)

Materials and Preparation

Materials Needed

For each participant:
- ❏ Bible and student textbook
- ❏ pencil

For each small group:
- ❏ four pieces of paper cut to 5-by-7-inch size
- ❏ colored pencils

Additional materials:
- ❏ one or more of your own family photo albums
- ❏ an empty 5-by-7-inch photo album

Other Preparation Steps

- ❏ Mark Luke 2:1–7 in the Bible that will be used in the opening prayer ritual.
- ❏ Choose two participants to process in with the Bible and a candle for the opening prayer ritual, providing directions as needed.

Background Reading

- Read the background page about Jesus Christ and his family on page 42 of the student textbook, including the suggested Bible passages.

Session Steps

A. Quick-Start Activity: Family Photo Album (5 minutes)

1. Place your family photo albums on a table near the board. **Write** the following on the board:

    ▶ Feel free to carefully look through my photo albums.

2. As the participants arrive, **instruct** them to follow the directions on the board.

B. Opening Prayer Ritual (5 minutes)

1. **Direct** the Bible bearer and candle bearer to take their places just outside the room or in the back of the room. **Gather** everyone else to stand around your prayer table. **Make** the Sign of the Cross and lead everyone in saying, "Let us remember that we are in the holy presence of God."

2. **Invite** the Bible bearer and candle bearer to silently process up to the prayer table and turn to face the group. The Bible bearer then **reads** the Scripture verse you have marked, Luke 2:1–7. When finished, the reader says, "The Word of the Lord." Everyone responds, "Thanks be to God." The Bible bearer and candle bearer then place the Bible and candle on the prayer table and go to their places.

3. Invite everyone to sit down. **Introduce** Jesus and his family in these or similar words:

   ▶ Today we will study Jesus and his family. The stories surrounding Jesus' family are both spectacular and ordinary. They are spectacular in showing God's amazing plan at work. They are ordinary in sounding much like our own family stories. The presence of the ordinary helps us to see ourselves in the story, and the spectacular encourages us to grow as a family, as we shall see in this passage.

C. Bible Story Sharing: The Escape to Egypt (10 minutes)

Note Alternative Option: Omit step C if you choose to have the participants read the background sheet in the student textbook during class. Instead, the participants would use this time to complete the reading. You may wish to use the methods outlined in Suggestions for Reading Together, in the introduction to this catechist guide.

1. **Direct** the participants to open their Bibles to Matthew 2:13–23. Provide help as needed but encourage the participants to try to find the passage on their own. **Read** the passage together. See the introduction in this catechist guide for different ways to do this.

2. **Lead** the group in a short reflection on the Bible passage. Encourage the participants to share their thoughts.

   ▶ Why did Joseph take Mary and Jesus to Egypt? *(Answer: An angel told him to flee because King Herod was seeking to kill Jesus.)*

   ▶ If you were Joseph, what might have gone through your mind on hearing the news from the angel?

   ▶ How do your parents or others who are responsible for your welfare protect you?

3. **Summarize** the meaning of this Bible passage in these or similar words:

   ▶ Imagine the horror Joseph and Mary must have felt when they heard that the king planned to kill their newborn child. Joseph was willing to uproot his family just to keep Jesus safe. Keeping you safe may not require such dramatic steps, but your parents or guardians make difficult decisions about your safety too. Sometimes just deciding to let you stay out later with friends or to let you chat online can involve issues of safety. No doubt, at times you will disagree with them on those decisions, but it may help to remember that as parents or guardians, just like Joseph and Mary, they have the responsibility to ensure your safety and well-being.

D. Review Student Textbook Activity Page (10 minutes)

Note Alternative Option: Omit step D–1 if you choose to have the participants complete the activity page at home after the session.

1. Ask the participants to **turn to the activity** on page 43 in the student textbook. Ask them to **check** their completed work as you review the answers. See the introduction in this catechist guide for suggestions on how to do this.

2. After checking the answers, **summarize** key aspects of Jesus and his family by **presenting the following points:**

   ▶ When the time is right, God sends his only Son, Jesus, who is both fully divine and fully human, into the world to conquer sin and death.

   ▶ Mary and Joseph willingly accept God's will and cooperate with God's plan to bring about Jesus' miraculous birth.

   ▶ From his birth, some view Jesus as a threat. Mary and Joseph even flee to Egypt rather than risk having King Herod kill their son.

   ▶ As a young person, Jesus stays behind in the Temple, already aware of his mission to do his Father's work.

E. Integration Activity: Jesus' Family Photo Album (25 minutes)

In this activity the participants will reflect on the purpose of a family photo album. Then they will explore stories from Jesus' childhood and develop family photos for those events. They will consider the similarities between their family and Jesus' family and how the Holy Family is an example to us all.

1. **Refer** to your photo albums from the Quick-Start Activity. Briefly go through a few of your favorite pictures and explain why you like them. Then **say** these or similar words:

   ▶ Family photo albums are record books that help us remember important events and people in our lives. Because cameras didn't exist when Jesus walked the earth, we have only the stories that were written down to describe the important events and people in his family's life. Today we are going to take the written words about Jesus as a child and create Jesus' family photo album.

2. **Place** the participants into small groups of two or three. Give each group four pieces of 5-by-7-inch paper and some colored pencils. Assign each group one of the following passages:

   - Luke 2:1–7 (Jesus Christ is born.)
   - Luke 2:8–25 (The shepherds and angels worship the baby Jesus.)
   - Matthew 2:1–12 (Visitors arrive from the East.)
   - Luke 2:21–38 (Jesus is named and presented in the Temple.)
   - Luke 2:41–52 (The boy Jesus teaches in the Temple.)

3. **Instruct** each group to read its passage and then develop and draw four photos that Mary or Joseph might have taken to remember the moment. Tell the groups to write on the back of each photo the names of the people in the picture and to provide a comment from Mary's or Joseph's perspective about what is going on in the picture.

4. Once the groups have completed their photos, **assemble** the photos in chronological order into the empty photo album. Then **share** the entire album with the class. Have the groups that drew each photo share a little about it.

5. Then **lead** a discussion, using these or similar questions:

   ▶ Based on the stories from Jesus' childhood, what can we learn about Jesus and his family?

   ▶ What about Jesus' childhood is similar to yours?

6. Then **conclude** with these or similar words:

   ▶ Although Jesus walked the earth two thousand years ago, some things about family never change. For example, Mary and Joseph celebrate the birth of their child. Visitors come to celebrate with them. They share their faith with their child. They seek to better understand Jesus as he grows up. We are fortunate to have the example of Jesus' family, also known as the Holy Family. They too have experienced the ups and downs of being a family.

F. Announcements and Closing Prayer (5 minutes)

1. Make any needed **announcements. Assign** the background page to read and the activity to fill out for the next session if you will have the participants work on this at home.

2. Close by **leading** the participants in a short prayer, perhaps like the following:

   ▶ God, thank you for the example of family you gave us in Mary, Joseph, and Jesus. We want to take this time to thank you for our own families.

Allow the participants to make their own prayers by saying:

   ▶ I now offer each of you an opportunity to offer a prayer for your own family.

Once those who wish to offer prayers have done so, conclude with the Lord's Prayer.

Chapter 20

Jesus' Teachings and Miracles

Session Focus

- The participants will learn key facts about Jesus Christ's teachings and miracles:
    - He teaches about love and the Kingdom of God.
    - He uses parables as a unique way to teach about God and the Kingdom.
    - He performs many healing miracles to demonstrate the power of God's love.
    - Faith is the only thing Jesus asks of those he heals.
- The participants will study stories of Jesus' healing miracles and reflect on key questions:
    - In the stories of the healing miracles, how important is having faith in Jesus?
    - Are there times when you can turn to Jesus for healing, having faith that you will receive what you need?

At a Glance

A. Quick-Start Activity: Make a Paper Clip Float (5 minutes)
B. Opening Prayer Ritual (5 minutes)
C. Bible Story Sharing: God and Possessions (10 minutes)
D. Review Student Textbook Activity Page (10 minutes)
E. Integration Activity: Miracle Bingo (25 minutes)
F. Announcements and Closing Prayer (5 minutes)

Materials and Preparation

Materials Needed

For each participant:

❑ Bible and student textbook

❑ pencil

❑ handout 20–A, "Miracle Bingo"

❑ coins or markers for bingo, at least nine

Additional materials:
- ❏ open box
- ❏ three bowls with water
- ❏ several paper clips
- ❏ small candies or other small bingo prizes

Other Preparation Steps

- ❏ Mark Mark 12:28–34 in the Bible that will be used in the opening prayer ritual.
- ❏ Choose two participants to process in with the Bible and a candle for the opening prayer ritual, providing directions as needed.
- ❏ Cut apart Bible passages on resource 20–A, "Bingo Passages," and put them in an open box.
- ❏ Practice floating a paper clip in water as described in part E, "Miracle Bingo."

Background Reading

- Read the background page about Jesus Christ's teachings and miracles on page 44 of the student textbook, including the suggested Bible passages.

Session Steps

A. Quick-Start Activity: Make a Paper Clip Float (5 minutes)

1. On a table, place a pile of paper clips and three bowls with water in them. Then **write** the following on the board:

   ▶ Using only the materials on the table, float one paper clip on the water.

2. As the participants arrive, **instruct** them to follow the directions on the board.

B. Opening Prayer Ritual (5 minutes)

1. **Direct** the Bible bearer and candle bearer to take their places just outside the room or in the back of the room. **Gather** everyone else to stand around your prayer table. **Make** the Sign of the Cross and lead everyone in saying, "Let us remember that we are in the holy presence of God."

2. **Invite** the Bible bearer and candle bearer to silently process up to the prayer table and turn to face the group. The Bible bearer then **reads** the Scripture verse you have marked,

Mark 12:28–34. When finished, the reader says, "The Word of the Lord." Everyone responds, "Thanks be to God." The Bible bearer and candle bearer then place the Bible and candle on the prayer table and go to their places.

3. Invite everyone to sit down. **Introduce** Jesus' teachings and miracles in these or similar words:

   ▶ Today we will study the teachings and miracles of Jesus Christ. Jesus is a remarkable teacher because his words and deeds follow what he teaches. Jesus teaches about love and shows remarkable love for all people. Jesus speaks of compassion and shows compassion through his many healing miracles. Most important, Jesus reminds the people of God's love and calls them to simply trust in God, as we shall see in this passage.

C. Bible Story Sharing: God and Possessions (10 minutes)

Note Alternative Option: Omit step C if you choose to have the participants read the background sheet in the student textbook during class. Instead, the participants would use the time to complete the reading. You may wish to use the methods outlined in Suggestions for Reading Together, in the introduction to this catechist guide.

1. **Direct** the participants to open their Bibles to Luke 12:22–31. Provide help as needed but encourage the participants to try to find the passage on their own. **Read** the passage together. See the introduction in this catechist guide for different ways to do this.

2. **Lead** the group in a short reflection on the Bible passage. Encourage the participants to share their thoughts.

   ▶ How are the birds and flowers taken care of? *(Answer: God provides for them. They do not have to do anything about food or clothing, and they are better off than kings.)*

   ▶ Because Jesus was talking to the disciples, do you think they worried more about food or clothing?

   ▶ What types of things have you worried about, only later to realize that God had already taken care of it for you?

3. **Summarize** the meaning of this Bible passage in these or similar words:

   ▶ Jesus teaches many things about love and God's care for us. In this passage, he focuses on the stress and worries that consume our time and energy. Jesus tells us that God does not want us to worry. Instead we should be concerned with fulfilling God's will and simply trust that God will take care of the rest. Next time you feel stressed, ask yourself if you are doing God's will. If so, then simply trust God to take care of the rest.

D. Review Student Textbook Activity Page (10 minutes)

Note Alternative Option: Omit step D–1 if you choose to have the participants complete the activity page at home after the session.

1. Ask the participants to **turn to the activity** on page 45 in the student textbook. Ask them to **check** their completed work as you review the answers. See the introduction in this catechist guide for suggestions on how to do this.

2. After checking the answers, **summarize** key aspects of Jesus Christ's teachings and miracles by **presenting the following points:**

    ▶ Jesus teaches about God's Kingdom, in which everybody acts out of love.

    ▶ Jesus uses parables, which are stories about everyday things with a twist at the end, to help people understand what the Kingdom of God is like.

    ▶ Jesus also performs miracles, many of which are healings. These miracles show God's care for all people and our need to care for one another.

    ▶ Through both Jesus' teachings and miracles, we learn that God desires us to love one another and place our faith in the power of God.

E. Integration Activity: Miracle Bingo (25 minutes)

In this activity the participants will consider the true nature of miracles. Then through a game of bingo, they will learn about the many stories in the Bible in which Jesus miraculously heals people.

1. **Ask** if any participants were able to get a paper clip to float on the water during the Quick-Start Activity. If so, ask them to explain how they did it. If not, turn your back to the participants so they cannot see what you are doing. Then take one paper clip and bend it open to make the shape of an *L*. Continuing to hide what you are doing, use the bent paper clip to gently lower another paper clip onto the surface of the water. The surface tension on the water should prevent the paper clip from sinking. Once you have a floating paper clip, turn and show the class. **Ask** them the following questions:

    ▶ Is this a miracle? *(Answer: No.)*

    ▶ How do you define a miracle? *(Answer: A miracle is something that can only be explained as a supernatural act of God.)*

Then **explain** that a floating paper clip is not a miracle, and show them how you did it. **Say** that the Gospels report many real miracles that Jesus performed, such as walking on water. We also have many stories of Jesus performing healing miracles, which the participants will explore through a game of bingo.

2. **Give** each participant a pencil, a copy of handout 20–A, "Miracle Bingo," and sufficient markers or coins for their playing cards. Tell them to write in each square a different quote on the bottom of the sheet. Once they have filled in their cards, give them the following instructions:

   ▶ You will randomly select a reading slip from the box.

   ▶ Everybody will look up the passage, and a volunteer will read it aloud.

   ▶ Check to see if you used the quote from that passage on your bingo card. If you did, mark the passage.

   ▶ We will keep repeating this until someone gets a bingo. If time permits, we will play several rounds.

   Begin playing bingo. You may wish to give candy or other small prizes to the winners.

3. After you have finished playing, **conclude** with these or similar words:

   ▶ Imagine the effect each of these miracles had on the people Jesus healed. From their encounters with Jesus, their lives were changed. Jesus never asked them for money. He just wanted them to have faith. We all have areas in our lives that need healing. We can remember Jesus' miraculous power to heal and simply have faith that he will help us. We know Jesus does not always grant us healing in the way or at the time we may think we need it. Part of our faith in Jesus is to simply trust his power to heal and his wisdom in how he uses that power.

F. Announcements and Closing Prayer (5 minutes)

1. Make any needed **announcements. Assign** the background page to read and the activity to fill out for the next session if you will have the participants work on this at home.

2. Close by **leading** the participants in a short prayer, perhaps like the following:

   ▶ Jesus, you taught about your wonderful Kingdom and how we are all called to love. Help us live our lives focused on your love. In a special way, we offer in prayer our loved ones who are sick or need your special healing.

   Allow the participants to mention those they would like to offer up in prayer. **Conclude** by saying:

   ▶ Lord we offer up all those we have mentioned and all those who have nobody to pray for them unless we pray. Amen.

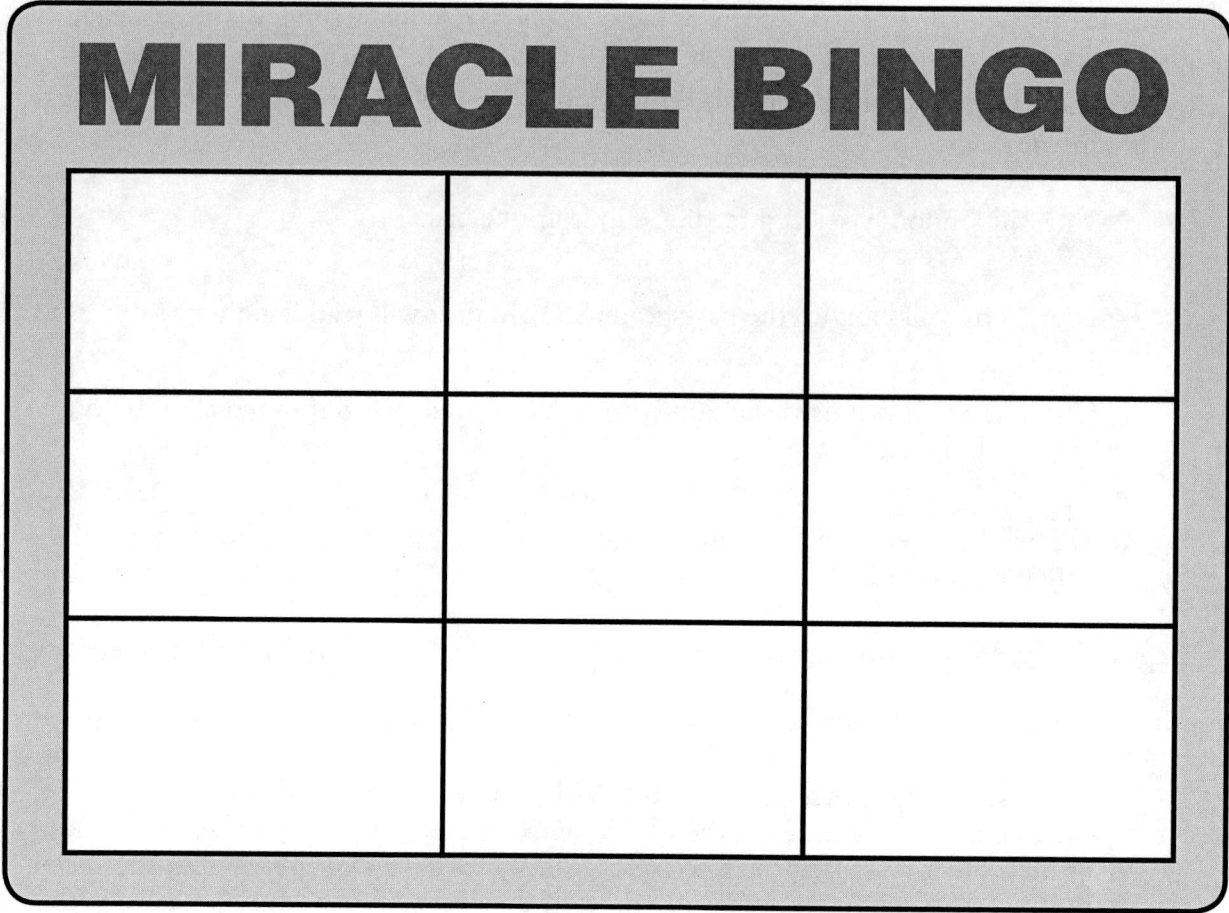

To prepare your bingo card, select nine quotations from those below and write them randomly in the bingo squares above.

"Dreaded skin disease"   "Ephphatha"

"Mother-in-law"   "Trees walking around"

"Herd of pigs"   "God's holy messenger"

"Pick up your bed"   "The dead man sat up"

"Musicians for the funeral"   "Legs and arms were swollen"

"Have mercy on us, Son of David"   "Your son will live"

"The man started talking"   "Pool"

"Touch the edge of his cloak"   "Come out!"

Bingo Passages

Cut out the passages below.

Matthew 8:1–4	Matthew 9:18–26	Mark 7:31–37	Luke 14:1–6
Matthew 8:14–15	Matthew 9:27–31	Mark 8:22–26	John 4:49–54
Matthew 8:28–34	Matthew 9:32–34	Luke 4:31–37	John 5:1–9
Matthew 9:1–7	Mark 6:53–56	Luke 7:11–17	John 11:38–44

Answer Key

Note that these quotes are taken from the Good News Translation (GNT). If you are using a different translation, inform the players that there may be minor differences in the translations and to therefore pick the quotes that best resemble the passage.

Matthew 8:1–4
"Dreaded skin disease"

Matthew 8:14–15
"Mother-in-law"

Mark 1:29–31
"Mother-in-law"

Matthew 8:28–34
"Herd of pigs"

Matthew 9:1–7
"Pick up your bed"

Matthew 9:18–26
"Musicians for the funeral"

Matthew 9:27–31
"Have mercy on us, Son of David"

Matthew 9:32–34
"The man started talking"

Mark 6:53–56
"Touch the edge of his cloak"

Mark 7:31–37
"Ephphatha"

Mark 8:22–26
"Trees walking around"

Luke 4:31–37
"Gods' holy messenger"

Luke 7:11–16
"The dead man sat up"

Luke 14:1–6
"Legs and arms were swollen"

John 4:49–54
"Your son will live"

John 5:1–9
"Pool"

John 11:38–44
"Come out!"

Resource 20–A: Permission to reproduce is granted. © 2010 by Saint Mary's Press.

Chapter 21

Jesus' Death and Resurrection

Session Focus

- The participants will learn key facts about Jesus Christ's death and Resurrection:
  - He willingly dies a painful death to save us, and we too shall be resurrected if we put our faith in him.
  - After his Resurrection, Jesus appears to the disciples and many others.
  - Jesus helps Thomas overcome his doubts about the Resurrection.
  - Forty days after his Resurrection, Jesus ascends into Heaven and now sits at God's right hand.
- The participants will study the last words of Jesus and reflect on key questions:
  - How do Jesus' words reflect the love and compassion he taught throughout his ministry?
  - How can we imitate Jesus, by acting lovingly toward those around us when we suffer?

At a Glance

A. Quick-Start Activity: Famous Last Words (5 minutes)
B. Opening Prayer Ritual (5 minutes)
C. Bible Story Sharing: Jesus and Thomas (10 minutes)
D. Review Student Textbook Activity Page (10 minutes)
E. Integration Activity: Jesus' Last Words (25 minutes)
F. Announcements and Closing Prayer (5 minutes)

Materials and Preparation

Materials Needed

For each participant:

❏ Bible and student textbook

❏ pencil

❏ colored pencils

❏ piece of paper cut to 4¾ by 9½ inches, folded in half to resemble a CD case

Other materials:
- ❏ easel-sized paper
- ❏ tape

Other Preparation Steps

- ❏ Mark Luke 23:44–46 in the Bible that will be used in the opening prayer ritual.
- ❏ Choose two participants to process in with the Bible and a candle for the opening prayer ritual, providing directions as needed.
- ❏ Write the title "Jesus' Last Words" on a sheet of easel-sized paper. Below it list the following passages:
    - Mark 15:33–36
    - Luke 23:32–34
    - Luke 23:39–43
    - Luke 23:44–46
    - John 19:26–27
    - John 19:28
    - John 19:29–30

Background Reading

- Read the background page about Jesus Christ's death and Resurrection on page 46 of the student textbook, including the suggested Bible passages.

Session Steps

A. Quick-Start Activity: Famous Last Words (5 minutes)

1. **Write** the following on the board:

    ▶ Here are some famous last words:
    "I die hard but am not afraid to go."
    "Is it the Fourth?"
    "I love you Sarah. For all eternity, I love you."

▶ If you knew you were about to die, what would you want your last words to be? Write your ideas below.

2. As the participants arrive, **instruct** them to follow the directions on the board.

B. Opening Prayer Ritual (5 minutes)

1. **Direct** the Bible bearer and candle bearer to take their places just outside the room or in the back of the room. **Gather** everyone else to stand around your prayer table. **Make** the Sign of the Cross and lead everyone in saying, "Let us remember that we are in the holy presence of God."

2. **Invite** the Bible bearer and candle bearer to silently process up to the prayer table and turn to face the group. The Bible bearer then **reads** the Scripture verse you have marked, Luke 23:44–46. When finished, the reader says, "The Word of the Lord." Everyone responds, "Thanks be to God." The Bible bearer and candle bearer then place the Bible and candle on the prayer table and go to their places.

3. Invite everyone to sit down. **Introduce** Jesus' death and Resurrection in these or similar words:

▶ Today we will study the death and Resurrection of Jesus Christ. His death is an incredibly painful way to die, yet by willingly suffering, Jesus takes on the sins of the world. Through his death and Resurrection, he conquers sin and death so that through him we may be resurrected into eternal life. Throughout his suffering, Jesus shows compassion, and he continues to do so after his Resurrection, as we shall see in this passage.

C. Bible Story Sharing: Jesus and Thomas (10 minutes)

Note Alternative Option: Omit step C if you choose to have the participants read the background sheet in the student textbook during class. Instead, the participants would use the time to complete the reading. You may wish to use the methods outlined in Suggestions for Reading Together, in the introduction to this catechist guide.

1. **Direct** the participants to open their Bibles to John 20:24–29. Provide help as needed but encourage the participants to try to find the passage on their own. **Read** the passage together. See the introduction in this catechist guide for different ways to do this.

2. **Lead** the group in a short reflection on the Bible passage. The following questions can help prompt discussion. Encourage all the participants to share their thoughts.

▶ What does Thomas say he needs to do to believe Jesus was raised from the dead? *(Answer: He said he actually had to touch the nail marks and wounds of Jesus.)*

▶ If you were Thomas, and the disciples told you they had seen Jesus, what might you have done?

▶ Have you ever doubted God or your faith? How did you handle those doubts? Do you still have doubts about some areas of faith?

3. **Summarize** the meaning of this Bible passage in these or similar words:

▶ Jesus has appeared to the disciples, yet Thomas doubts Jesus has really risen from the dead. Thomas demands physical proof before he is willing to believe. When Jesus appears again, he willingly offers what Thomas needs. Sometimes we have to live with doubts until things become clear. When we doubt like Thomas, we can pray for the gift of faith and remember Jesus' compassion toward Thomas and how he gave the gift needed to help Thomas' faith grow.

D. Review Student Textbook Activity Page (10 minutes)

Note Alternative Option: Omit step D–1 if you choose to have the participants complete the activity page at home after the session.

1. Ask the participants to **turn to the activity** on page 47 in the student textbook. Ask them to **check** their completed work as you review the answers. See the introduction in this catechist guide for suggestions on how to do this.

2. After checking the answers, **summarize** key aspects of Jesus Christ's death and Resurrection by **presenting the following points:**

▶ Although Jesus is innocent, he is convicted of blasphemy and suffers one of the most painful deaths imaginable—crucifixion. By doing so, Jesus takes the sins of the world upon himself.

▶ That the Messiah needs to suffer and die surprises many during Jesus' time. The Gospels give us many details about Jesus' suffering, death, and Resurrection to help others understand the role of the Messiah.

▶ On the third day after Jesus dies on the cross, he rises from the dead and appears to his disciples and many others.

▶ Forty days after Jesus rises from the dead, he ascends into Heaven. He is now seated at God's right hand until he returns.

E. Integration Activity: Jesus' Last Words (25 minutes)

In this activity the participants will explore the last words Jesus speaks while dying on the cross. Despite enormous pain and suffering, Jesus shows great compassion and courage while dying for us. Jesus' words can serve as an example to us on how to respond to our own suffering.

1. **Refer** to the quotations on the board from the Quick-Start Activity. **Ask** volunteers to share their "last words." Then tell them that all three quotations were by U.S. presidents:

    ▶ "I die hard but am not afraid to go" is from President George Washington, who died on December 14, 1799.

    ▶ "Is it the Fourth?" is from President Thomas Jefferson, who died on July 4, 1826.

    ▶ "I love you Sarah. For all eternity, I love you" is from President James K. Polk, speaking to his wife when he died in 1849.

    Then **say** these or similar words:

    ▶ Often a person's last words can reflect something about that person's character or what the person considered important. Today we will explore the last words of Jesus.

    Ask the participants to take out their Bibles. Distribute colored pencils and a piece of paper cut to 4¾ by 9½ inches and folded in half, one for each participant. Then on a wall, tape the easel-sized paper titled "Jesus' Last Words."

    Give the participants the following instructions:

    ▶ You will create and decorate a case for a CD that we will title "Jesus' Last Words."

    ▶ Create a song title for each Scripture passage on the large sheet of paper, expressing what you think Jesus meant. Put the titles on the back of the case.

    ▶ Inside the CD case, write out lyrics for one of the songs.

2. After sufficient time, **invite** volunteers to share their CD cases with the group.

3. Then **ask:**

    ▶ When you are sick or in pain, how do you react? Do you treat people kindly, or do you say unkind things? How can Jesus' behavior on the cross be an example to us on how to handle pain or suffering?

4. After the participants have shared, **conclude** by saying:

   ▶ The amazing thing about Jesus' last words is that during incredible suffering, he still displays the compassion and love he showed during his ministry. His last words cover a range of emotions and reveal a lot about his character. His cry about being forsaken by God shows the anguish he endures for our sake. His compassion can be heard in his prayer asking God to forgive those who are crucifying him and in his promise of paradise to a repentant criminal. His lifelong desire to fulfill God, the Father's, plan for him can be heard when he offers his spirit up to God and declares, "It is finished." If you find yourself suffering for any reason, you can recall the words of Jesus and remember how he chooses to show love and compassion.

F. Announcements and Closing Prayer (5 minutes)

1. Make any needed **announcements. Assign** the background page to read and the activity to fill out for the next session if you will have the participants work on this at home.

2. Close by **leading** the participants in a short prayer, perhaps like the following:

   ▶ Lord Jesus, you humbly suffered and gave your life so we can have eternal life with you and our Heavenly Father. Give us the courage to do the right thing, even if it means we must suffer. We ask this in your name. Amen.

Chapter 22

Peter

Session Focus

- The participants will learn key facts about Peter:
  - He is a disciple of Jesus who later becomes known as the first Pope.
  - He often displays great faith in Jesus.
  - His weaknesses often get in the way of his great faith.
  - He boldly preaches the Good News to the world.
- The participants will study parts of Peter's life and reflect on key questions:
  - What strengths and weaknesses do you have, and how can God work through you to do great things, as he worked through Peter?
  - How can understanding your own strengths and weaknesses help you see what role Jesus calls you to fulfill in your life?

At a Glance

A. Quick-Start Activity: Finding a Job (5 minutes)
B. Opening Prayer Ritual (5 minutes)
C. Bible Story Sharing: Peter Names Jesus the Messiah (10 minutes)
D. Review Student Textbook Activity Page (10 minutes)
E. Integration Activity: Job Opening (25 minutes)
F. Announcements and Closing Prayer (5 minutes)

Materials and Preparation

Materials Needed

For each participant:
- ❏ Bible and student textbook
- ❏ pencil
- ❏ scissors
- ❏ a 4¼-by-11-inch strip of paper

For each small group:
- a 4¼-by-11-inch strip of paper
- markers

Additional materials:
- employment sections from newspapers
- a sheet of easel-sized paper with the heading "Want Ads" across the top
- tape
- one additional 4¼-by-11-inch strip of paper for you

Other Preparation Steps

- Mark Matthew 4:18–20 in the Bible that will be used in the opening prayer ritual.
- Choose two participants to process in with the Bible and a candle for the opening prayer ritual, providing directions as needed.

Background Reading

- Read the background page about Peter on page 48 of the student textbook, including the suggested Bible passages.
- If you are using *Breakthrough! The Bible for Young Catholics*, read the article "Peter the Rock," located near Matthew 16:13–17.

Session Steps

A. Quick-Start Activity: Finding a Job (5 minutes)

1. Have available copies of the employment section from your local newspapers, as well as scissors for each student. **Write** the following on the board:

    ▶ It is time to get a job. Look through the employment section of the newspapers and pick out a job you would like to do. Cut out the ad and keep it with you for later.

2. As the participants arrive, **instruct** them to follow the directions on the board.

B. Opening Prayer Ritual (5 minutes)

1. **Direct** the Bible bearer and candle bearer to take their places just outside the room or in the back of the room. **Gather** everyone else to stand around your prayer table. **Make** the Sign of the Cross and lead everyone in saying, "Let us remember that we are in the holy presence of God."

2. **Invite** the Bible bearer and candle bearer to silently process up to the prayer table and turn to face the group. The Bible bearer then **reads** the Scripture verse you have marked, Matthew 4:18–20. When finished, the reader says, "The Word of the Lord." Everyone responds, "Thanks be to God." The Bible bearer and candle bearer then place the Bible and candle on the prayer table and go to their places.

3. Invite everyone to sit down. **Introduce** Peter in these or similar words:

   ▶ Today we will study Peter, the first leader of the Church, known today as the first Pope. Peter is making a living by fishing when Jesus calls him to be a disciple. Peter has a strong faith in Jesus, but sometimes his weaknesses get in the way. Peter is a great leader who understands who Jesus really is, as we shall see in this passage.

C. Bible Story Sharing: Peter Names Jesus the Messiah (10 minutes)

Note Alternative Option: Omit step C if you choose to have the participants read the background sheet in the student textbook during class. Instead, the participants would use the time to complete the reading. You may wish to use the methods outlined in Suggestions for Reading Together, in the introduction to this catechist guide.

1. **Direct** the participants to open their Bibles to Matthew 16:13–17. Provide help as needed but encourage the participants to try to find the passage on their own. **Read** the passage together. See the introduction in this catechist guide for different ways to do this.

2. **Lead** the group in a short reflection on the Bible passage. If you are using *Breakthrough! The Bible for Young Catholics,* consider reading to the group the article "Peter the Rock," located near this story. The following questions can help prompt discussion. Encourage all the participants to share their thoughts.

   ▶ What question does Jesus ask, and what is Peter's reply? *(Answer: Jesus asks, "Who do you say I am?" Peter replies that Jesus is the Messiah.)*

   ▶ If you were Peter, how would you have felt having Jesus tell you that what you said could have come only from God?

   ▶ An important part of spreading our faith is being able to explain who Jesus is to a friend. If a friend asked you, "Who is Jesus?" how would you respond?

3. **Summarize** the meaning of this Bible passage in these or similar words:

   ▶ Have you ever noticed that whenever something interesting or unusual happens at school, the story gets quickly passed around? Apparently, the same type of thing was happening with Jesus. People were talking about Jesus and his teachings and miracles. Knowing this, Jesus asks the disciples what they have heard people saying about him. Hearing their responses, Jesus realizes that the crowds don't yet understand who he is, so he asks what the disciples think. Peter boldly states that Jesus is the Messiah, the Savior promised by God. Jesus praises him for his response. Faith in Jesus may come up in conversation when we are with our friends. It is important for us to know about our faith so we can share it openly when the opportunity arises.

D. Review Student Textbook Activity Page (10 minutes)

Note Alternative Option: Omit step D–1 if you choose to have the participants complete the activity page at home after the session.

1. Ask the participants to **turn to the activity** on page 49 in the student textbook. Ask them to **check** their completed work as you review the answers. See the introduction in this catechist guide for suggestions on how to do this.

2. After checking the answers, **summarize** key aspects of Peter's life by **presenting the following points:**

   ▶ Peter and his brother, Andrew, are making their living by fishing when Jesus asks them to become his disciples.

   ▶ Peter is the first to say that Jesus is the Messiah. Jesus replies that God has given Peter this truth. He declares that Peter will serve as the foundation of the Church.

   ▶ Peter shows human weakness by denying Jesus three times while Jesus is being questioned after his arrest. Peter is sorry for his choice, and Jesus forgives him.

   ▶ After Jesus' Resurrection, Peter becomes the leader of the early Church and is known as our first Pope.

E. Integration Activity: Job Opening (25 minutes)

In this activity the participants will consider Peter's qualifications for his role as the first leader of the Church. Peter often shows great faith, but sometimes he shows great weakness. Like Peter we all display both faith and weakness at times. Through learning about Peter, the participants can gain assurance that God can use them for great things too.

1. **Instruct** the participants to take out the want ads they cut out during the Quick-Start Activity. Then **invite** volunteers to share which jobs they chose for themselves. Ask what qualities and experience they would need to do the jobs selected. Also ask what attracted them to the positions.

   Then **say** these or similar words:

   ▶ Every job requires certain personal qualities, as well as previous related experience. The same is true for Peter's role as the first leader of the Church. When Jesus picks

Peter to be the leader of the Church, he obviously sees that Peter has certain necessary qualities and experiences. So your job today will be to work in small groups to write a help-wanted ad for the first leader of the Church, Peter. Your ad must include a listing of the qualifications for the position, preferred work experience, and salary or compensation—which may be something other than money. You will be assigned a passage about Peter, so write your ad as if you were looking for an applicant who would fit Peter's profile from your passage. For example, if your passage talks about Peter walking on water, then your ad should include being able to have great trust and walk on water.

Place the participants into small groups of three or four. Give each group markers and a 4¼-by-11-inch strip of paper to write their ad on. Tell them to write their ad on the paper vertically; it should resemble ads from the newspapers. **Assign** each group one of the following passages:

- Matthew 14:22–33 (Jesus walks on the water.)
- Matthew 16:18–23 (Peter's declaration about Jesus, and Jesus rebukes him.)
- John 1:35–42 (Jesus chooses his disciples.)
- John 21:15–19 (Jesus forgives Peter.)
- Acts 2:14,22–23 (Peter preaches to the crowds.)
- Acts 10:36–42 (Peter speaks to Cornelius.)

Hang the easel-sized paper with the title "Want Ads" on the board. **Invite** the groups to present their ads. Ask them to share how their passages influenced the ads they wrote. After each group finishes, have it tape its ads on the large "Want Ads" sheet. By the end, this sheet should resemble a newspaper employment section.

Then using one more 4¼-by-11-inch sheet of paper, **lead** the participants in writing a want ad that combines the main qualities of Peter as found in the different groups' ads. Once you have completed the ad, tape it with the other ads.

Then **give** each participant a 4¼-by-11-inch slip of paper and **say** these or similar words:

▶ God called Peter to take on an incredible job for Jesus. Jesus has a job or role for each of us. Take a moment to think about the type of job you want to do for Jesus. It may be a paid job, a volunteer ministry, or a way of acting toward others. Think about your own strengths and weaknesses, and the gifts and talents you will need to perform that role. Then on the slip of paper, write a brief job description for that role. Once you have completed it, tape it on the large sheet with our want ads for Peter's job.

Conclude with these or similar words:

> ▶ Peter is an interesting choice for the Church's first leader. At times Peter displays enormous faith and conviction about Jesus. At other times he shows the same weaknesses and sinfulness we all experience at times. Perhaps it is the balance of both the strong and the weak in Peter that makes him such a great leader. Jesus' selection of Peter shows that each of us has the potential to do great things for Jesus.

F. Announcements and Closing Prayer (5 minutes)

1. Make any needed **announcements. Assign** the background page to read and the activity to fill out for the next session if you will have the participants work on this at home.

2. Close by **leading** the participants in a short prayer, perhaps like the following:

> ▶ God, your servant Peter showed both great faith and weakness. Often we do the same. Help us to remember Peter and have the assurance that although we are imperfect, we still may do great things in your name. Amen.

Chapter 23

Mary Magdalene

Session Focus

- The participants will learn key facts about Mary Magdalene:
  - Jesus drives out demons from her.
  - She follows Jesus, listening to his teachings.
  - She stands by Jesus' side while he dies on the cross.
  - She is known as the Apostle to the Apostles.
- The participants will study the story of Jesus' appearance to Mary Magdalene and reflect on key questions:
  - How does Mary Magdalene model seeking Jesus, finding him in unexpected ways, and sharing the Good News?
  - How can you, as young people, imitate Mary Magdalene's faith?

At a Glance

A. Quick-Start Activity: Images (5 minutes)
B. Opening Prayer Ritual (5 minutes)
C. Bible Story Sharing: The Crucifixion of Jesus (10 minutes)
D. Review Student Textbook Activity Page (10 minutes)
E. Integration Activity: Mary's Example (25 minutes)
F. Announcements and Closing Prayer (5 minutes)

Materials and Preparation

Materials Needed

For each participant:
- ❏ Bible and student textbook
- ❏ pencil
- ❏ sheet of aluminum foil, large enough to be pressed over the participant's face

For each group:
- ❑ sheet of paper

Additional materials:
- ❑ tape

Other Preparation Steps

- ❑ Mark Luke 8:1–3 in the Bible that will be used in the opening prayer ritual.
- ❑ Choose two participants to process in with the Bible and a candle for the opening prayer ritual, providing directions as needed.

Background Reading

- Read the background page about Mary Magdalene on page 50 of the student text book, including the suggested Bible passages.

Session Steps

A. Quick-Start Activity: Images (5 minutes)

1. On a table make available the sheets of aluminum foil and tape. **Write** the following on the board:

   ▶ Take one sheet of foil and carefully press it against your face so it makes an image of your features. Then tape your image to the wall.

2. As the participants arrive, **instruct** them to follow the directions on the board.

B. Opening Prayer Ritual (5 minutes)

1. **Direct** the Bible bearer and candle bearer to take their places just outside the room or in the back of the room. **Gather** everyone else to stand around your prayer table. **Make** the Sign of the Cross and lead everyone in saying, "Let us remember that we are in the holy presence of God."

2. **Invite** the Bible bearer and candle bearer to silently process up to the prayer table and turn to face the group. The Bible bearer then **reads** the Scripture verse you have marked, Luke 8:1–3. When finished, the reader says, "The Word of the Lord." Everyone responds, "Thanks be to God." The Bible bearer and candle bearer then place the Bible and candle on the prayer table and go to their places.

3. Invite everyone to sit down. **Introduce** Mary Magdalene in these or similar words:

   ▶ Today we will study Mary Magdalene, who is a devoted follower of Jesus. Although she has had a troubled past, she meets Jesus and begins to follow him as he wanders the countryside, teaching. Perhaps the two words that best describe Mary Magdalene are "faithful" and "courageous." She was faithful to Jesus and his teachings. She was courageous in her desire to support him, as we shall see in this passage.

C. Bible Story Sharing: The Crucifixion of Jesus (10 minutes)

Note Alternative Option: Omit step C if you choose to have the participants read the background sheet in the student textbook during class. Instead, the participants would use the time to complete the reading. You may wish to use the methods outlined in Suggestions for Reading Together, in the introduction to this catechist guide.

1. **Direct** the participants to open their Bibles to John 19:16–30. Provide help as needed but encourage the participants to try to find the passage on their own. **Read** the passage together. See the introduction in this catechist guide for different ways to do this.

2. **Lead** the group in a short reflection on the Bible passage. The following questions can help prompt discussion. Encourage all the participants to share their thoughts.

   ▶ Where is Mary Magdalene while Jesus is dying on the cross? *(Answer: Mary Magdalene is with Jesus' mother, Mary, and several other women standing at the foot of the cross.)*

   ▶ If you were Mary Magdalene, would it have been easy or hard for you to stand at the foot of the cross? Why?

   ▶ What are ways we can be a friend like Mary Magdalene and stand by our friends' sides when they are suffering?

3. **Summarize** the meaning of this Bible passage in these or similar words:

   ▶ Mary Magdalene shows incredible courage to stand by Jesus' side while he hangs on the cross. Many other followers have run away and hidden, but Mary Magdalene stays with Jesus through thick and thin. It must be unbelievably difficult to stand there and see Jesus in so much pain. Likewise, it must be scary knowing the crowd could turn on her at any minute because she is his follower. Seeing someone we care about suffer can be difficult, but those are the times a loved one may need us the most. When we find ourselves in that situation, we can pray for guidance and strength to be a courageous and faithful friend like Mary Magdalene.

D. Review Student Textbook Activity Page (10 minutes)

Note Alternative Option: Omit step D–1 below if you choose to have the participants complete the activity page at home after the session.

1. Ask the participants to **turn to the activity** on page 51 in the student textbook. Ask them to **check** their completed work as you review the answers. See the introduction in this catechist guide for suggestions on how to do this.

2. After checking the answers, **summarize** key aspects of Mary Magdalene's life by **presenting the following points:**

   ▶ Mary Magdalene has had a troubled past, and Jesus even drives several demons out of her.

   ▶ She becomes a devoted follower of Jesus. Along with several other women, she travels the countryside, listening to Jesus teach.

   ▶ While Jesus dies on the cross, Mary Magdalene bravely stands by his side.

   ▶ While visiting Jesus' tomb, she becomes the first to encounter the Risen Christ, who tells her to announce to the Apostles that he has risen. For this, she is known as the Apostle to the Apostles.

E. Integration Activity: Mary's Example *(25 minutes)*

In this activity the participants will reflect on Mary Magdalene's encounter with Jesus near the tomb. They will consider how she seeks Jesus, finds him but doesn't recognize him at first, and shares the Good News with others. Then the participants will develop skits representing ways they as young people can be people of faith like Mary Magdalene.

1. **Refer** to the aluminum foil images on the wall from the Quick-Start Activity. Randomly point to some images and **ask** the class to guess whose face it is. Tell them not to guess if it is their own face.

Then **say** these or similar words:

   ▶ Mary Magdalene has an experience where she does not fully recognize someone she cares about very much. Let us listen to her story.

Read John 20:11–18. Then **lead** a discussion using these or similar questions:

   ▶ What questions does Jesus ask Mary Magdalene when he first speaks to her? *(Answer: He asks her why she is crying. He also asks whom she is looking for.)*

   ▶ Who does Mary think Jesus is before she recognizes him? *(Answer: She thinks Jesus is the gardener.)*

   ▶ What does Mary Magdalene do at the end of the passage? *(Answer: She tells the disciples she has seen the risen Lord.)*

Then **say** these or similar words:

> ▶ This story of Mary Magdalene gives us a good example of how to be a person of faith. Mary Magdalene does three things:
>
> - She actively seeks Jesus.
> - She ends up finding him but in an unexpected way.
> - She shares the Good News with others.

2. **Place** the participants into three groups. Give each group a sheet of paper. Assign each group one of the three ways listed above that Mary Magdalene models faith. Ask the groups to brainstorm ways they, as young people, can be more like Mary Magdalene based on their assigned example. Tell them to choose a note taker to write down their ideas. Once they have a list of ideas, the groups will develop a skit to present their best idea.

   After sufficient time, **invite** the groups to present their skits.

   Then **conclude** with these or similar words:

   > ▶ As your skits showed, there are many ways you, as young people, can show your faith like Mary Magdalene. By seeking Jesus, seeing him even in unexpected ways, and sharing the Good News, you too can be a person of faith. Just look at the faces you taped to the wall. Those are the faces of people of faith.

F. Announcements and Closing Prayer (5 minutes)

1. Make any needed **announcements. Assign** the background page to read and the activity to fill out for the next session if you will have the participants work on this at home.

2. Close by **leading** the participants in **a short prayer**, perhaps like the following:

   > ▶ God, Mary Magdalene chose to journey with Jesus all the way to the cross and through the Resurrection. Her faith is an example to us. Please give us the faith we need to seek you, find you in unexpected ways, and share the Good News about you. Amen.

Chapter 24

Paul

Session Focus

- The participants will learn key facts about Paul:
  - He originally persecutes the followers of Jesus by seeking to imprison them or have them executed.
  - The Risen Jesus miraculously appears to Paul, and Paul immediately changes his ways and becomes a follower of Jesus.
  - Paul travels all over the Roman world, risking his own life to teach and preach about Jesus.
  - New Testament letters provide a record of Paul's teachings.
- The participants will study Paul's writings on the Church as one body with many parts and reflect on key questions:
  - Why does the Church require a diversity of people with a diversity of gifts all working together?
  - Where do your own gifts fit into the work of the Church, and how can you build on those gifts?

At a Glance

A. Quick-Start Activity: Going Without (5 minutes)
B. Opening Prayer Ritual (5 minutes)
C. Bible Story Sharing: Paul's Conversion (10 minutes)
D. Review Student Textbook Activity Page (10 minutes)
E. Integration Activity: One Body, Many Parts (25 minutes)
F. Announcements and Closing Prayer (5 minutes)

Preparation and Materials

Materials Needed

For each participant:
- ❏ Bible and student textbook
- ❏ pencil
- ❏ strip of fabric the participants can tie around their limb in the Quick-Start Activity

For each small group:
- ❑ sheet of easel-sized paper
- ❑ markers

Additional materials:
- ❑ box

Other Preparation Steps

- ❑ Mark Romans 8:35–39 in the Bible that will be used in the opening prayer ritual.
- ❑ Choose two participants to process in with the Bible and a candle for the opening prayer ritual, providing directions as needed.
- ❑ Make individual slips of paper with the following phrases on them for the Quick-Start Activity, enough for one slip for each participant—you can duplicate or add to the list if necessary:

  - You cannot use your eyes.
  - You cannot use your mouth to talk.
  - You cannot use your left hand.
  - You cannot bend your left elbow.
  - You cannot use your right hand.
  - You cannot bend your right elbow.
  - You cannot use your right foot.
  - You cannot bend your right knee.
  - You cannot use your left foot.
  - You cannot bend your left knee.

Background Reading

- Read the background page about Paul on page 52 of the student textbook, including the suggested Bible passages.

Session Steps

A. Quick-Start Activity: Going Without (5 minutes)

1. In a box near the board, **place** the slips of paper with the directions about body parts. Next to it make available enough strips of material for each participant. **Write** the following on the board:

▶ Draw a slip of paper from the box. As a reminder, have a friend gently tie a strip of fabric around the part of your body mentioned on the slip. Don't tie it too tightly!

2. As the participants arrive, **instruct** them to follow the directions on the board.

B. Opening Prayer Ritual (5 minutes)

1. **Direct** the Bible bearer and candle bearer to take their places just outside the room or in the back of the room. **Gather** everyone else to stand around your prayer table. **Make** the Sign of the Cross and lead everyone in saying, "Let us remember that we are in the holy presence of God."

2. **Invite** the Bible bearer and candle bearer to silently process up to the prayer table and turn to face the group. The Bible bearer then **reads** the Scripture verse you have marked, Romans 8:35–39. When finished, the reader says, "The Word of the Lord." Everyone responds, "Thanks be to God." The Bible bearer and candle bearer then place the Bible and candle on the prayer table and go to their places.

3. Invite everyone to sit down. **Introduce** Paul in these or similar words:

    ▶ Paul is an unusual choice for one of the greatest missionaries the Church has ever seen. Paul is first known as Saul, who persecutes Christians by actively seeking to imprison them and hand them over for execution. God has other plans for Paul. Through a miraculous encounter with Jesus, Paul changes his heart and ways, as we shall see in this passage.

C. Bible Story Sharing: Paul's Conversion (10 minutes)

Note Alternative Option: Omit step C if you choose to have the participants read the background sheet in the student textbook during class. Instead, the participants would use the time to complete the reading. You may wish to use the methods outlined in Suggestions for Reading Together, in the introduction to this catechist guide.

1. **Direct** the participants to open their Bibles to Acts 9:1–19. Provide help as needed but encourage the participants to try to find the passage on their own. **Read** the passage together. See the introduction in this catechist guide for different ways to do this.

2. **Lead** the group in a short reflection on the Bible passage. The following questions can help prompt discussion. Encourage all the participants to share their thoughts.

    ▶ What happens to Paul, known as Saul at that time, on his journey near Damascus? *(Answer: Jesus suddenly appears to him and asks Saul why he is persecuting Jesus. Then Saul becomes blind and has to be led into Damascus.)*

    ▶ If you were Paul, what would have been the scariest part of your conversion? What would have been the most peaceful part? Why?

▶ Sometimes conversion, or turning one's heart toward God, can be an "all of a sudden" event like Saul's. Other times it can simply happen quietly and slowly over time. What are some ways we can open or prepare our hearts for God to work on them?

3. **Summarize** the meaning of this Bible passage in these or similar words:

▶ Paul, or Saul, has actively sought to imprison the Christians and hand them over for execution. Yet God chooses him to be one of the greatest missionaries Christianity has ever seen. His conversion shows us how dramatic a change people can make once they open their hearts to Christ. Every day we are called, like Paul, to open our hearts to Christ and work toward being more faithful followers of Jesus.

D. Review Student Textbook Activity Page (10 minutes)

Note Alternative Option: Omit step D–1 if you choose to have the participants complete the activity page at home after the session.

1. Ask the participants to **turn to the activity** on page 53 in the student textbook. Ask them **to check** their completed work as you review the answers. See the introduction in this catechist guide for suggestions on how to do this.

2. After checking the answers, **summarize** key aspects of Paul's life by **presenting the following points:**

▶ Paul is a Jewish leader who is well known for actively seeking to imprison or kill Christians.

▶ While traveling to round up more Christians, Paul has a dramatic conversion experience where the Risen Jesus appears to him. Paul is soon baptized and becomes a follower of Jesus.

▶ Paul travels all over the Roman world, spreading the Gospel. He helps found many churches and teaches countless people, both Jews and Gentiles, about Jesus.

▶ We have a record of his travels and teachings from many letters that are now part of the New Testament.

E. Integration Activity: One Body, Many Parts (25 minutes)

In this activity the participants will discuss the experiences they have had during the session, starting with the Quick-Start Activity, of not being able to use one of their body parts. Then in small groups, they will explore Paul's writings about the Church as one body in Christ by creating posters based on the passage and relating it to the Church today. They will consider the role of their own gifts in the Church and ways they can improve those gifts.

1. **Invite** volunteers to share how the session has been for them without the use of one part of their bodies. Then **ask** the following questions:

    ▶ Was there something you wanted to do but realized you could not?

    ▶ Did you find another way to do it, or did you just not do it at all?

    ▶ Did any of you help someone else out? How and why?

2. Then **say** these or similar words:

    ▶ Paul wrote about the Church and how all its different parts, the people who make up the Church, work together. He compares the Church to how the body works. So let us examine what Paul said.

    Place the participants into small groups of three to four. Give each group a sheet of easel-sized paper and some markers. Assign each group one of the following body parts: foot, hand, ear, or eye. Tell them to **read** 1 Corinthians 12:12–31. They will **create a poster** by drawing a person, making their assigned body part overly large. Next to their assigned body part, they will describe its normal physical function and then describe who or what type of work done in the Church may be represented by that body part. (The participants may use the list of ministries Paul provides in the passage as a starting point.)

3. After sufficient time, **invite** each group to present its poster. Then **lead** a discussion, using these or similar questions:

    ▶ What is the main point Paul makes about different body parts and the Church? *(Answer: Each person in the Church has different gifts, and we all need to respect the differences and work together as one.)*

    ▶ Of the four body parts Paul mentions, which one do you see yourself as most? Why?

    ▶ What would you need to do to be more effective as one of the body parts?

4. Then **conclude** with these or similar words:

    ▶ Paul envisions a Church where everybody works together and respects one another's unique gifts. We are called to strive for that same goal, by respecting and valuing the work of others. We can also build on our own gifts and willingly use them to build up Christ's Church here on earth.

F. Announcements and Closing Prayer (5 minutes)

1. Make any needed **announcements. Assign** the background page to read and the activity to fill out for the next session if you will have the participants work on this at home.

2. Close by **leading** the participants in a short prayer, perhaps like the following:

    ▶ Lord Jesus, give us the courage to proclaim your word as Paul so boldly did. Help us to truly live as one body in you. Amen.

Chapter 25

Priscilla and Aquila

Session Focus

- The participants will learn key facts about Priscilla and Aquila:
  - They are a Jewish couple who fled Rome.
  - They meet Paul and become Christians.
  - They travel with Paul to help spread the Good News.
  - They use their own home as a meeting place for the Church in Ephesus.
- The participants will study the story of Priscilla and Aquila's teaching of Apollos and reflect on key questions:
  - What are some stories about the Bible people you have learned during the course?
  - How can you, as young people, share your faith in words or deeds, as Priscilla and Aquila shared their faith?

At a Glance

A. Quick-Start Activity: Building a Campfire (5 minutes)
B. Opening Prayer Ritual (5 minutes)
C. Bible Story Sharing: Paul Greets Priscilla, Aquila, and Their Community (10 minutes)
D. Review Student Textbook Activity Page (10 minutes)
E. Integration Activity: Sharing Campfire Stories (25 minutes)
F. Announcements and Closing Prayer (5 minutes)

Materials and Preparation

Materials Needed

For each participant:
- ❏ Bible and student textbook
- ❏ pencil

Additional materials:
- ❏ materials to make a pretend campfire: logs or simulated logs, stones (or simulated stones) to surround them, red and yellow construction paper or plastic wrap to imitate a fire, flashlight to place in the middle to represent firelight

- ❏ sleeping bags to be spread out for seating
- ❏ optional: two-person tent, set up to help set the scene
- ❏ additional flashlights for the participants to share
- ❏ the Bible People pictures they drew during session 1 on salvation history

Other Preparation Steps

- ❏ Mark Acts 18:1–4 in the Bible that will be used in the opening prayer ritual.
- ❏ Choose two participants to process in with the Bible and a candle for the opening prayer ritual, providing directions as needed.

Background Reading

- Read the background page about Priscilla and Aquila on page 54 of the student text book, including the suggested Bible passages.
- If you are using *Breakthrough! The Bible for Young Catholics*, read the article "Side by Side," located near Romans 16:3–5.

Session Steps

A. Quick-Start Activity: Building a Campfire (5 minutes)

1. **Place** the materials for a pretend campfire in the middle of the room. These materials may include logs (or simulated logs, such as cardboard rolls from paper towels), stones (or construction paper loosely crumpled with corners taped together), red and yellow construction paper or plastic wrap, a flashlight, and sleeping bags. **Set up** a small tent near the fire if you choose to use this additional prop. Then **write** the following on the board:

   ▶ Using the materials provided, construct a campfire in the middle of the room. Place the flashlight in the middle of the campfire to make it appear to be lit. Place the sleeping bags around the fire.

2. As the participants arrive, **instruct** them to follow the directions on the board.

B. Opening Prayer Ritual (5 minutes)

1. **Direct** the Bible bearer and candle bearer to take their places just outside the room or in the back of the room. **Gather** everyone else to stand around your prayer table. **Make** the Sign of the Cross and lead everyone in saying, "Let us remember that we are in the holy presence of God."

2. **Invite** the Bible bearer and candle bearer to silently process up to the prayer table and turn to face the group. The Bible bearer then **reads** the Scripture verse you have marked, Acts 18:1–4. When finished, the reader says, "The Word of the Lord." Everyone responds, "Thanks be to God." The Bible bearer and candle bearer then place the Bible and candle on the prayer table and go to their places.

3. Invite everyone to sit down. **Introduce** Priscilla and Aquila in these or similar words:

    ▶ Today we will study Priscilla and Aquila, a married couple who openly shared their faith in Jesus. They became Christians after meeting a new friend, Paul. They traveled with Paul and worked to found more churches. Their desire to spread the Good News was matched by generosity and hospitality, as we shall see in this passage.

C. Bible Story Sharing: Paul Greets Priscilla, Aquila, and Their Community (10 minutes)

Note Alternative Option: Omit step C if you choose to have the participants read the background sheet in the student textbook during class. Instead, the participants would use this time to complete the reading. You may wish to use the methods outlined in Suggestions for Reading Together, in the introduction to this catechist guide.

1. **Direct** the participants to open their Bibles to Romans 16:3–5. Provide help as needed but encourage the participants to try to find the passage on their own. **Read** the passage together. See the introduction in this catechist guide for different ways to do this.

2. **Lead** the group in a short reflection on the Bible passage. If you are using *Breakthrough! The Bible for Young Catholics,* consider reading to the group the article "Side by Side," located near this story. The following questions can help prompt discussion. Encourage all the participants to share their thoughts.

    ▶ Based on this passage, what can you tell me about Priscilla and Aquila? *(Answer: They are "fellow workers" of Paul who have risked their lives to help Paul and use their own home as a place for the local faith community to meet.)*

    ▶ If you were Priscilla or Aquila and part of an illegal faith community, would you be willing to use your home as the meeting place for your small community, especially if it meant putting your family in danger?

    ▶ Clearly, because of their faith in Jesus Christ, Priscilla and Aquila welcomed people. How does your faith in Jesus Christ affect how you try to make others feel welcome in your home?

3. **Summarize** the meaning of this Bible passage in these or similar words:

    ▶ The faith, courage, and willingness to open the doors of their home earn Priscilla and Aquila the honor of being personally mentioned in Paul's letters. This couple was an ordinary, hard-working couple who simply desired to live their faith. We too can be like Priscilla and Aquila by striving to welcome in the name of Christ every person we meet.

D. Review Student Textbook Activity Page (10 minutes)

Note Alternative Option: Omit step D–1 if you choose to have the participants complete the activity page at home after the session.

1. Ask the participants to **turn to the activity** on page 55 in the student textbook. Ask them to **check** their completed work as you review the answers. See the introduction in this catechist guide for suggestions on how to do this.

2. After checking the answers, **summarize** key aspects of Priscilla and Aquila's life by **presenting the following points:**

    ▶ Priscilla and Aquila are a Jewish couple who have been forced to flee Rome.

    ▶ They are tent makers, and when they arrive in Corinth, they become friends with Paul, who is also a tent maker.

    ▶ After meeting Paul they become Christians and work with Paul to spread the faith. They even risk their own lives for Paul.

    ▶ They help establish and lead the faith community in Ephesus by allowing the community members to meet in their home.

E. Integration Activity: Sharing Campfire Stories (25 minutes)

In this activity the participants will reflect on how Priscilla and Aquila sat around with Apollos and shared with him their stories about Jesus. The participants will then do their own storytelling around a "campfire" by sharing the stories of the many people they have studied during this course. They will reflect on ways they can share with others what they have learned.

1. **Invite** the participants to sit on the sleeping bags around the campfire they constructed during the Quick-Start Activity. Hand out the flashlights and turn on the one in the campfire. Dim the lights in the room. **Ask** the participants what comes to mind when they think of campfires and camping in tents. **Invite** volunteers to share experiences they have had of sitting around campfires. Mention how tenting often provides wonderful experiences of sitting at the campfire and sharing stories. Then **say:**

    ▶ As you already have learned, Priscilla and Aquila are tent makers like Paul. Apparently they are also good storytellers when it comes to sharing the story of Jesus Christ. Listen to a time they share the story of their faith.

2. **Read** Acts 18:24–26. Then **lead** a discussion using these or similar questions:

    ▶ What information about Jesus is Apollos mistaken about? *(Answer: He knows only about John's form of baptism, not Jesus'.)*

    ▶ What do Priscilla and Aquila do after they hear Apollos speak? *(Answer: They meet privately with Apollos and share with him stories and teachings about Jesus.)*

    Then **say:**

    ▶ Today all of you are going to be like Priscilla and Aquila, and I am going to be Apollos. I am going to show you pictures of people from our faith, and you will share their stories with me.

3. Select five pictures the participants drew during the first session, on salvation history, choosing characters that interested the participants most. One by one **hold up** the pictures and **lead** a brief review of each person by asking the participants to explain who each person is and how that person showed faith in God through words or deeds.

4. Once you have reviewed a few of the Bible people, **ask** the participants to brainstorm ways they, as young people, can spread their faith in words or deeds.

5. Then **conclude** with these or similar words:

    ▶ As our final Bible people, Priscilla and Aquila are wonderful examples of what it means to spread the story of our faith. They open their home and invite others in just to tell them about the amazing things God has done through Jesus Christ. We are called to take all we have learned about God and his people and share it freely with everybody we meet. We can share it in words or in deeds, but we must share it.

F. Announcements and Closing Prayer (5 minutes)

1. Make any needed **announcements**.

2. Close by **leading** the participants in a short prayer, perhaps like the following:

    ▶ God, we praise you for this time you have given us over the past several weeks to learn about many amazing people of faith. As we continue on our own journeys of faith, help us remember not just the wonderful examples of faith we have in the Bible but also the amazing love you have for each of us. Amen.

Appendix: Answer Key

Salvation History

After the students have reviewed the time line provided in this book, ask the students to be creative and draw a picture representing an event or two from the time line. If the students are stumped, you might suggest some of the following:

- Primeval History—Creation to 2000 BC
  + tower, boat and rain
- Egypt and the Exodus—1700 BC to 1250 BC
  + broken chains, law tablets, mountain
- Kingdoms of Judah and Israel—1050 BC to 587 BC
  + temple, cityscape, crown, prophet's sign
- Life of Jesus Christ—AD 1 to AD 33
  + heart, cross, tomb with an open door
- Patriarchs—2000 BC to 1700 BC
  + handshake, map
- Settling the Promised Land—1250 BC to 1050 BC
  + judge's gavel, flag on land
- Exile and Return—587 BC to AD 1
  + chains, countdown numbers 50–1
- Early Christian Church—AD 33 to AD 100
  + *Good News* paper, pulpit, map of Italy with Rome marked, dove

Introduction to the Old Testament

ANSWERS TO OLD TESTAMENT QUESTIONS 1–10
1. 46
2. Genesis
3. Malachi
4. Obadiah
5. Psalms
6. Pentateuch, History, Wisdom, Prophets
7. Genesis, Exodus, Leviticus, Numbers, Deuteronomy
8. Proverbs
9. History, Prophets
   Wisdom, Prophets

COMPLETED SENTENCE
Israelites chosen people

Adam and Eve

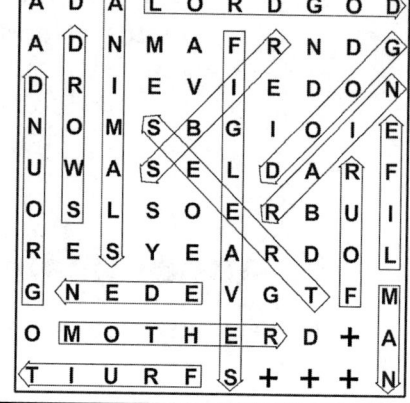

WORDS HIDDEN IN WORD SEARCH
1. RAIN
2. GROUND
3. EDEN
4. LIFE
5. FOUR
6. MAN
7. GOOD
8. ANIMALS
9. RIBS
10. FRUIT
11. FIG LEAVES
12. TREES
13. MOTHER
14. LORD GOD
15. SWORD

FILL-IN ANSWER: ADAM AND EVE DISOBEYED GOD.

Noah

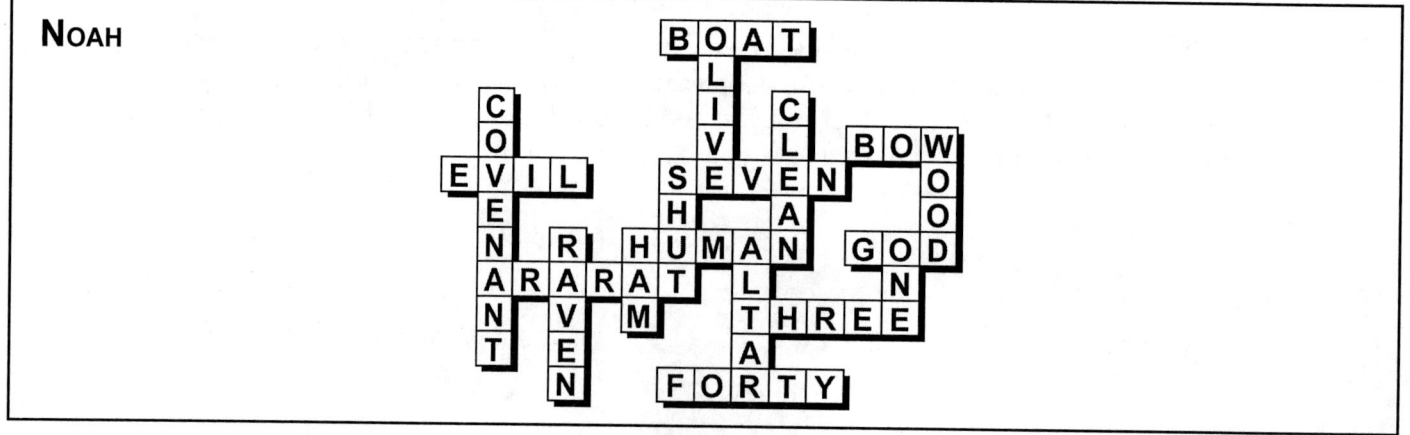

Appendix: Answer Key   **149**

Abraham and Sarah

EVENT ORDER WITH LETTERS TO BE INSERTED IN BLANK SPACES AT BOTTOM

(1) 7   b and e   (4) 8   s   (7) 1   b   (10) 4   e   (13) 5   d and h
(2) 10 e   (5) 9   i and d (8) 14 h   (11) 12 A   (14) 11 s
(3) 3   r and i   (6) 13 r and a (9) 6   i and m (12) 2   u

FILL-IN ANSWER: BURIED HIM BESIDE SARAH

Moses

EVENT ORDER WITH LETTERS TO BE INSERTED IN BLANK SPACES AT BOTTOM

(1) 9   a and f   (4) 10 r   (7) 2   a   (10) 6   f and a (13) 3   c and e
(2) 12 e   (5) 7   c and e (8) 4   t   (11) 11 i   (14) 5   o
(3) 13 n   (6) 1   f   (9) 14 d   (12) 8   a and s

FILL-IN ANSWER: FACE TO FACE AS A FRIEND

Joshua

WORDS HIDDEN IN WORD SEARCH

1. MOUNTAIN   5. SEVEN   9. KINGS
2. WISDOM   6. LAW   10. LORD
3. JERICHO   7. STAND STILL 11. EPHRAIM
4. JORDAN   8. ISRAEL

FILL-IN ANSWER: MOSES APPOINTED JOSHUA HIS SUCCESSOR.

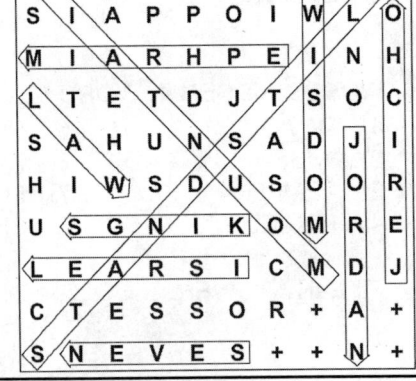

Samson

THE MOTHER OF SAMSON WAS NOT TO DRINK WINE

| THE | MOTH | ER | OF | SA | MSON | WAS |
| NOT | TO | DRIN | K WI | NE |

SAMSON TORE APART A LION WITH HIS BARE HANDS

| SAMS | ON T | ORE | APAR | T A | LION |
| WIT | H HI | S BA | RE H | ANDS |

THE LORD MADE SAMSON STRONG ENOUGH TO BREAK THE ROPES THAT HELD HIM

THE	LOR	D MA	DE S	AMSO	N ST
RONG	EN	OUGH	TO B	REAK	THE
ROP	ES T	HAT	HELD	HIM

SAMSON KNOCKED DOWN A BUILDING AND KILLED THE PHILISTINES

SAMS	ON K	NOCK	ED D	OWN	A BU
ILDING	AND K	ILLED	THE PH
ILIS	TINE	S

Ruth

"IF" - "THEN" STATEMENTS WITH LETTERS TO BE USED IN BLANK SPACES AT BOTTOM

1 = G	5 = T	9 = N	13 = T
2 = R	6 = G	10 = D	14 = H
3 = E	7 = R	11 = M	15 = E
4 = A	8 = A	12 = O	16 = R

FILL-IN ANSWER: Great-Grandmother

David

ANALOGIES
1. Jonathan is to Saul as Amnon is to **DAVID**. (son to father)
2. Kish is to Saul as **JESSE** is to David. (father to son)
3. Samuel is to Saul as **SAMUEL** is to David. (one who anoints)
4. Jonathan is to Michal as Absalom is to **TAMAR**. (brother to sister)
5. Nabal is to Abigail as Uriah is to **BATHSHEBA**. (first husband to wife of David)
6. Saul is to the Ammonites as David is to the **PHILISTINES**. (conqueror to conquered)
7. Jerusalem is to Solomon as **BETHLEHEM** is to David. (hometown to person)
8. Nathan is to a prophet as Joab is to a **GENERAL/ARMY COMMANDER**. (person to vocation)

Solomon

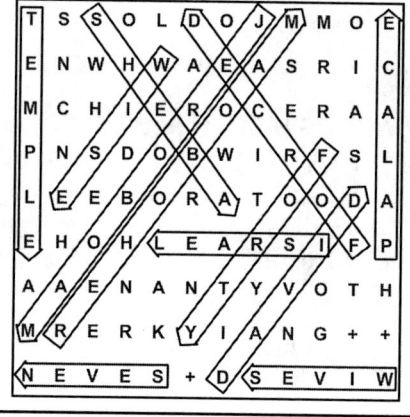

WORDS HIDDEN IN WORD SEARCH
1. DAVID
2. WISE
3. TEMPLE
4. ISRAEL
5. SEVEN
6. PALACE
7. FORCED
8. SHEBA
9. WIVES
10. JEROBOAM
11. FORTY
12. REHOBOAM

FILL-IN ANSWER: SOLOMON WAS RICHER AND WISER THAN ANY OTHER KING.

Isaiah

Appendix: Answer Key

EZEKIEL

WORDS HIDDEN IN WORD SEARCH
1. EXILES
2. WHEELS
3. SCROLL
4. SIDE
5. HAIR
6. HOLE
7. GLORY
8. COVENANT
9. EVIL
10. JERUSALEM
11. SHEPHERD
12. DRY BONES
13. TEMPLE

FILL-IN ANSWER: Ezekiel was a prophet to Judah and was taken into exile in Babylon.

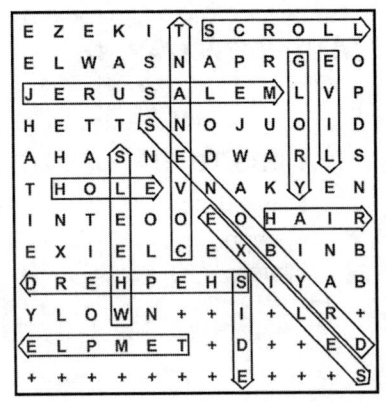

EZRA AND NEHEMIAH

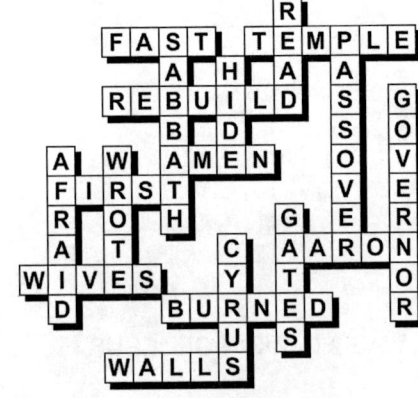

THE MACCABEES

ANSWERS TO STATEMENTS
1. Mattathias
2. Judas
3. Antiochus
4. Rededicated
5. Eleazar
6. Burn
7. Rome
8. Galilee
9. Simon

In what year did the Jews win their battle for freedom? 170

What year is that in the current calendar? 142 BC

INTRODUCTION TO THE NEW TESTAMENT

ANSWERS TO NEW TESTAMENT QUESTIONS 1–8
1. 27
2. Matthew
3. Revelation
4. Acts of the Apostles
5. 2 John has the fewest number of verses of any book in the Bible, and 3 John has the fewest number of words of any book in the Bible.
6. Matthew, Mark, Luke, John
7. (Varies)
8. Acts of the Apostles

COMPLETED SENTENCE
Jesus Christ first Christians

Mary of Nazareth

Answers to Statements

1. Simeon
2. Joseph
3. Water
4. Bethlehem
5. Elizabeth
6. Nazareth
7. Gabriel
8. Holy Spirit
9. Blessed

John the Baptist

WORDS HIDDEN IN WORD SEARCH

(1) ZECHARIAH
(2) ELIZABETH
(3) JORDAN
(4) HEAD
(5) HEROD
(6) GOOD NEWS
(7) PRISON
(8) DESERT
(9) SINS
(10) LAMB OF GOD
(11) DISCIPLES
(12) CAMELS HAIR

FILL-IN ANSWER: JOHN THE BAPTIST WAS A COUSIN OF JESUS.

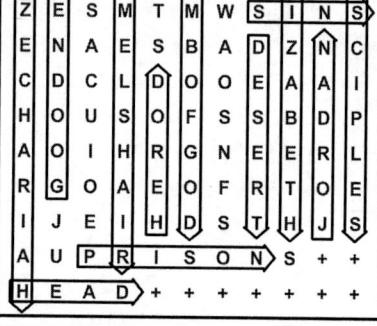

Jesus and His Family

Jesus' Teachings and Miracles

Matthew 6:31–33	EVERYTHING
Matthew 13:44–46	TREASURE
Matthew 25:34–40	OTHERS
Mark 10:23–27	RICH
Matthew 8:5–13	SERVANT
Mark 2:1–12	ROOF
Luke 18:35–43	FAITH
Luke 4:31–37	AUTHORITY

The parables and miracles of Jesus teach us that . . .

faith is necessary

. . . for entering the Kingdom of God.

Appendix: Answer Key **153**

Jesus' Death and Resurrection

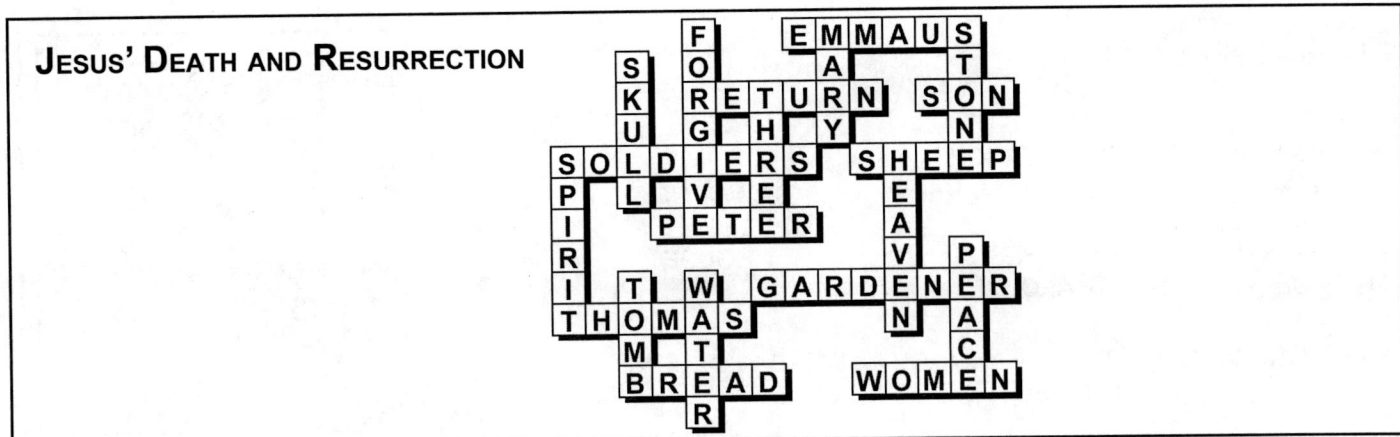

Peter

Mary Magdalene

ANSWERS TO STATEMENTS

1. Mother
2. Appeared
3. Gardener
4. Lord
5. Apostles
6. Angels
7. Spices
8. Stone
9. Seven

Paul

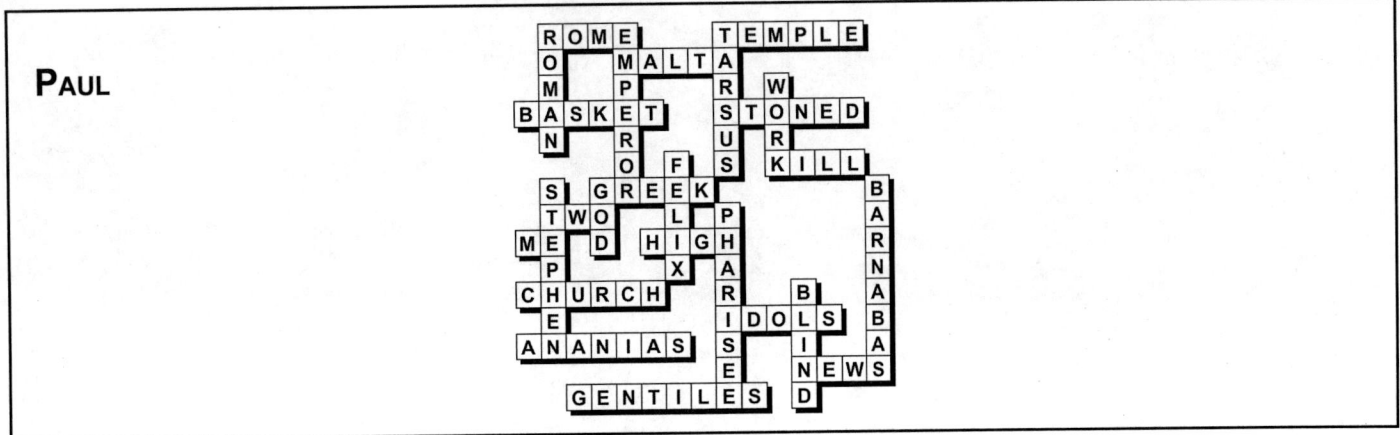

Priscilla and Aquila

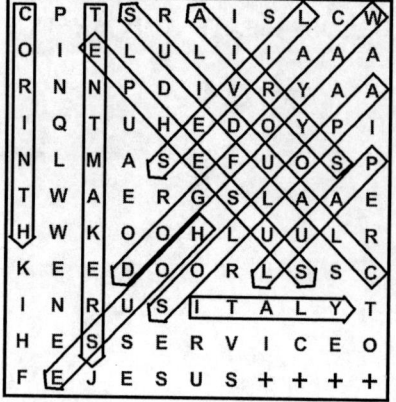

WORDS HIDDEN IN WORD SEARCH
(1) ITALY
(2) CLAUDIUS
(3) CORINTH
(4) PAUL
(5) TENT MAKERS
(6) SYRIA
(7) EPHESUS
(8) APOLLOS
(9) WAY OF GOD
(10) LIVES
(11) HOUSE

FILL-IN ANSWER: PRISCILLA AND AQUILA WERE WORKERS IN THE SERVICE OF JESUS.